NEB

MAYA

LAND OF THE TURKEY AND THE DEER

Other Books About Major Cultures of the World

Land of the Pharaohs, by Leonard Cottrell

The Chinese Way of Life, by Lin Yutang

The Byzantines, by Thomas C. Chubb

The Arabs, by Harry B. Ellis

The Sun Kingdom of the Aztecs, by Victor W. von Hagen

MAYA

LAND OF
THE TURKEY AND THE DEER

by

VICTOR W. VON HAGEN

Illustrated by Alberto Beltrán

COLLINS ⊙ WORLD

For

Bettina

the youngest of the

von Hagen tribe

Library of Congress Cataloging in Publication Data

Von Hagen, Victor Wolfgang, 1908-
Maya, land of the turkey and the deer.
Bibliography: p.
Includes index.
SUMMARY: Recreates Mayan life as it was before the
coming of the Spaniards including its history, culture,
and achievements.
1. Mayas — Juvenile literature. [1. Mayas]
I. Beltrán, Alberto.   II. Title.
[F1435.V74   1977]   972   76-30839
ISBN 0-529-03567-7 lib. bdg.

CONTENTS

Pronunciations for unfamiliar words
are given in the Index

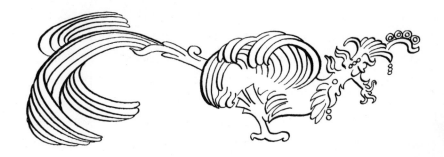

THE BEGINNINGS

THE MAYAS endured from about 2000 B.C. until 1697 A.D. not merely as a people, but also as a civilization.

For any people or culture to have existed in the same place for almost four thousand years is a long, long time in history. Few peoples have ever done this. And it is all the more remarkable, since the Mayas developed from a very primitive, prehistoric people. They originated among nomadic tribes who came out of Asia more than twenty-five thousand years ago, crossing over the Bering Strait—then a dry-land bridge—to North America. These nomads were the first inhabitants of the New World. Then, because of changes on the earth's surface, the land bridge sank, leaving only the tops of mountains—which are now islands—to mark its original location. The people who crossed over never returned to the lands of their origin.

These nomads were hunters and were probably following animals when they crossed the land bridge. In this new world, they continued their hunt for animals and gradually spread over the land. When they were not hunting or fishing, they ate wild native plants and harvested roots and grain. In time, they became farmers, developing corn, potatoes, peanuts, squash, and tomatoes out of the wild plants. These became the food-base of their society.

About the year 2000 B.C. a group of these new "Americans" reached the area that now comprises Guatemala, Chiapas, and Yucatán. They settled this region, continuing to live there from that date until 1697 A.D. when the last representatives of the old Maya culture, the Itzá-Mayas, were wiped out by Spanish soldiers. In the long interval between, the Mayas filled the jungles and the plain of the area with their stone-built cities.

In time, they became masters of nature. They built towering pyramids that rose above the tallest trees of the jungle; one at the great Maya city of Tikal is 227 feet high. They felled the trees, cut a wide path, and built stone-laid roads. These roads stretched out in all directions, thereby enabling all of the Maya cities to be in touch with each other. They invented a form of writing and developed an intricate calendar. They formed a clan-society which was based on tradition.

Nowhere else in the Americas was architecture, sculpture, painting, and weaving so wonderfully done. Yet the Mayas had no beasts of burden—their pack animals were they themselves. Not having the idea of the wheel, they had to carry everything on their backs. Until very late in their culture, they had no metal, and then only gold and soft copper. Therefore, they had to use stone. Stone axes felled the great trees, stone mallets chipped softer rock, stone chisels cut stone. Sculptures

as delicately wrought as those done by other peoples who had hard-metal tools were sculpted only with stone celts.

These were their handicaps, and yet they carved out of their jungles a place in human memory by building cities which, even today, astound man.

At one time during their history—about 800 A.D.—there were more than 3 million Mayas. Their homes were everywhere about—in the highlands, in the humid jungles, and on the high banks of plunging rivers. Then they were destroyed. Their cities —and there were many—became concentrated on the flat lowlands of Yucatán.

At the time our story begins, the Mayas had already been living in their own land for 3,515 years.

It is the time of the Maya 2 Ahau 8 Mac, but in the time of the Spaniard it is February, 1515.

Out in the semidarkness of the channel that sweeps between Yucatán and the Isle of Cozumel, is a small fleet of dugout canoes. . . .

THE MOON GODDESS

THE ANGRY WAVES, lashed by current and wind, spilled over the sides of the lead canoe and over the man sitting in the bow, wetting his parrot-feather headdress and smearing his red-and-black body paint. Still, the features of his proud face did not change. He kept his eyes fixed on the distant shoreline of Yucatán and was as quiet as the priest, squatting behind him, was noisy. As the large dugout plunged in the waves the latter constantly chanted prayers to the water gods.

The priest's robe was made of white cloth that had been beaten out of bark, and it was bare of any ornament except a small row of shells sewed around the bottom. The lobes of his ears had been slit and widened, and in them he wore large spool-shaped earrings. His long black hair was stained by the blood of sacrificial victims.

10

On both sides of the sixty-foot-long dugout were rows of paddlers—sixteen to each side—who paddled in unison. They squatted back on their haunches as in prayer. They were naked except for a loincloth of woven cotton which wrapped around their waist and was pulled up between their legs. This was called an *ex*, and it was worn by all Maya men. Their hair, usually worn long and braided, was now wrapped around the top of their heads, to be out of the way. Their only ornament was a small mirror of black obsidian glass which came, as every Maya knew, from the outpourings of volcanoes. All Maya men wore such mirrors attached to their braids by a string. For whenever they had nothing else to do, they looked at themselves. They pulled out facial hair, which they disliked; or they looked at themselves while they painted their faces. Now there was no time to look into mirrors. Between the rows of paddlers were huddled the passengers, soaked by the sea spray. High waves lashing against the sides of the canoe lifted it partly out of the sea. The water pouring over the high gunwales, swished back and forth inside the boat with each movement of the waves. The passengers were terribly frightened. Some chanted with the priest as he asked the water gods to curb their anger and let the people return to Tulum, their home, in safety.

Even though the sea was high, the voyagers were alert to attack. At the bottom of other canoes, warriors squatted, tightly gripping their long spears. Carib Indians, who lived on islands in the Caribbean Sea, were a fierce people, said to eat the flesh of their captives, and they sailed their canoes all over the ocean waters.

The voyage to and from Cozumel Island, which lay on the open Caribbean Sea, had never been easy. No one could foretell when the sea would become as it was now, wild and furi-

ous, or when the Carib would appear. Yet at least once in his
life every Maya was expected to go to the sacred shrines on
Cozumel, where Maya priests attended the oracles. For Cozumel was the home of Ixchel, the moon goddess, who was very
powerful. When women wanted children they went to the island
to pray at her shrines, for she was the goddess of childbirth.
She watched over mothers and their children, and she was the
patroness of weaving as well. She was also the goddess of
medicine.

"Bail, Ah Tok, Bail!"

It was the chieftain in the bow of the lead canoe who spoke.
The young boy who lay huddled at his mother's feet instantly
picked up the broken half of a calabash and began to bail. As
fast as he scooped up the water, more waves poured over the
gunwales, but he never stopped. Like all Maya boys, Ah Tok
wore only an *ex* and sandals of deer hide. His hair, just beginning to grow long, was brushed back from his face, showing
the characteristic flat forehead. For all Mayas of good family
had their heads flattened. When Ah Tok lay strapped to his

cradle, his mother had put his head between two tightly bound
boards. As an infant's skull is soft, the forehead could be flattened in a few months' time. No one knew why this was done,
only that it was custom. Some said that, since all Mayas carried
cargoes on their backs, and strapped to their foreheads, it made
carrying easier. Ah Tok's grandfather, who at festivals wore a
magnificent feather headdress on his sloping head, said: "We
flatten our heads because it gives us a noble air."

As Ah Tok bailed he now and then glanced back at the dark
outline of Cozumel. It had been his first visit to the famous
shrine. But then, he was just thirteen, and boys of his age were
not expected to make the pilgrimage. He looked at his mother,
who sat erect and unafraid, tightly holding his brother, whom
she had wrapped in a woven cotton manta. It was because of
the boy's illness that she had gone to Cozumel to ask Ixchel to
give him health.

A shout came from one of the canoes. The lights of Tulum
had been sighted. Torches made of pine resin had been placed

on the walls in expectation of the pilgrims' arrival. Soon they would be safely home.

So the moon goddess had protected them! It was for this very reason that Ah Tok had burned drops of scented copal resin before her shrine. And this, too, was the reason his uncle had cut his own tongue with an obsidian knife and let drops of blood fall on a piece of bark cloth. These had been their offerings.

The moon goddess was only one of many gods. More than other boys his age, Ah Tok could remember most of their names, because his father was a *tupil,* an official of Tulum. And his grandfather was keeper of the sacred books, so Ah Tok was taught more than others. The heavens were divided into thirteen sections, with a different god residing in each. There were four gods who held up the heavens, and to aid them on each side was a silk-cotton tree. (There were many silk-cotton trees in the land of the Mayas. Each year when the pods burst open, all the children ran out to gather the kapok—the silky fibers around the seeds of the tree—and use it to stuff pillows and mattresses.)

The world, Ah Tok's grandfather said, rested on the back of a large crocodile. And this might be true, for sometimes the earth shook—and this was probably caused when the crocodile moved.

There were sky gods, earth gods, and water gods. Each profession—hunter, warrior, saltmaker—had its own god. Those who kept bees had their own goddess, too. When the time came to pay her honor, the beekeepers made a fermented drink from honey, which they drank at the festival. The merchants had their god, and the warriors . . .

But the most important one to those who lived on the sea was the moon goddess, who also regulated the sea and took care of the tides. Ah Tok called her: "Our Mother." But his grandfather, who could read the old Maya writing, called her: "Our Grandmother."

When a Maya planted seed, he had to say aloud the names of the earth gods. As corn was put in the ground a prayer was said: "Oh, God! I make you my offering. I am sowing here my cornfield. Watch it for me, guard it for me; let nothing happen to it from the time I sow until I harvest it . . ." And there were so many other gods. It was good that the priests knew them all and could consult their painted books. For how could the unknowing Indians possibly know . . .

Now the walls of the city of Tulum could be seen. Guards, holding torches that spluttered in the night, ran toward the small harbor.

The city stood on a high limestone cliff, one hundred feet above the lash of the sea. Waves rolled in and broke furiously against the natural or artificial walls that protected it. The only entrance to Tulum from the sea was a small beach. When the canoes moved into position they were sent forward by the waves. As soon as each came to a halt in the sand, the warriors rushed down to pull the canoe to safety.

Ah Tok, with all the others, had arrived home safely.

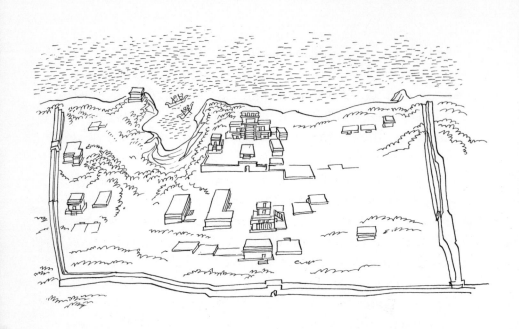

TULUM, THE WALLED CITY

TULUM was a very old city, in spite of its modern look. The temple walls were always freshly painted in blue and white. The murals on these walls—pictures that showed the Maya gods in conversation—were repainted each year so that they seemed ever new. In the center of the city stood several ancient time-markers, each higher than a man and each carved from a single piece of stone. One marker showed a figure of a chieftain, with an enormous headdress of feather-plumes; below him were rows of symbols in Maya writing which read: "This was erected in the Maya time 8 Ahau 13 Ceh."

Ah Tok's grandfather explained the meaning of the marker to the boy. The date "8 Ahau 13 Ceh" (433 A.D.) meant that Tulum was now over a thousand years old. In other years it had been called Zama, or City of the Dawn. It had been so

16

named, because as anyone could see, the Great Temple—which had its back toward the sea—received the first flush of dawn. Later when the city was walled, as it was now, people began to call it Tulum, which means just that. There were, of course, older Maya cities in the deep jungles inland, beyond Tulum. But these were now only shadow cities, visited only by priests. The jungles had grown over them.

Although small, Tulum was important. There were numerous other smaller cities strung along the shore both south and north of it. All were connected by a wide stone road, called *sacbe*. Only people of importance lived in Tulum. There were not many more than fifty buildings within its walls. Other Mayas, who were farmers or fishermen, lived scattered throughout the land.

The wall surrounding Tulum was one of Ah Tok's earliest memories. How many times he and his friends had walked along it and played on it! Over 3,600 feet long, it began where the cliffs met the sea and continued all around the city, forming a rectangle to the edge of the other cliff. In places it was very wide, as much as twenty feet. The boys could jump across the open parts, which were the narrow gateways to the city. There were five such gateways. One faced west in the direction of the great cities, such as Chichén Itzá and Uxmal. Two others opened to the south, leading to the road that went toward the great bay of Zamabac in the Maya province of Chetumal, famous for its honey and giant dugout canoes. One opened to the beach which gave access to the sea, and the last faced the jungle. All these passageways were so narrow that not more than one man could pass through at a single time. This made them easy to defend.

Hardly a day passed that an expedition did not enter Tulum

through one of its gateways. When they saw the long line of
carriers approach, the guards pounded their drums, and almost
instantly the walls would be filled with warriors, spears in hand.
If the visitors were friendly, the gates were opened, and one by
one the slave-carriers would come into the city and go down
to the small beach.

The slaves on these trading expeditions had close-cropped
hair, and wore neither paint nor emblems. They were either Indians who had been captured in battle, or Mayas who had lost
their rights because they had committed a crime against their
clan. Cargo was tied onto a slave's back by means of a rope

which passed around the forehead. A grown man could carry at least ninety pounds an entire day, and even a boy like Ah Tok was able to carry thirty pounds. He had often done so while helping his father harvest the corn crop.

Trading expeditions were led by the *ploms,* the merchants who were called the "possessed men" because they possessed very many things regarded as luxuries. They were usually fatter than most Mayas, not only because they did not till the fields, but also because—like the chieftains—they were often carried in litters along the broad highways. In Tulum they lived in houses alongside that of the city governor.

Since it was so well protected, Tulum was a safe place to store cargo. All sorts of things were traded there: rolls of woven cotton cloth, or manta; pottery wrapped in straw matting; honey in pots; salt carried in heavy sacks made from the fiber of the henequen plant. In addition, there were feathers and jade, shells and topaz, which the merchants gathered in large amounts. When all was safe within the walls, a fleet of seagoing canoes came up from Chetumal. As soon as they were loaded, the boats sailed to places unknown to the ordinary Maya. Months later they would return with gold, pearls, and other treasures from lands to the south.

In the center of Tulum were the temples. The largest and most important of these, the Great Temple, was surrounded by a court. Fronting the court were the houses in which the priests lived. The *batab,* who was the governor of the city, also lived in this area. A little further from the main temple were other

warrior

plom

batab   *holpop*

smaller temples. The Temple of the Diving God (so-called because he seemed to be plunging to earth) was painted blue. Around this temple were the houses of other officials. One of the larger houses, painted red and black, belonged to the *nacom,* or war captain. Every two years the heads of the clans, a union of families, sat down to elect the most valiant of their number to be the war captain. They treated him almost as if he were a god, and dressed in a beautifully woven manta, he was carried about in a litter. When he came by, Ah Tok saluted the *nacom* by touching the ground with stiff arms, then putting some of the dust of the earth on his forehead as he stood erect again. It was the custom he had learned from the older men.

The houses of other officials, counted as the "minor ones," also stood near this temple. One of these was the house of the *holpop,* or judge. The Mayas sat on woven mats, and *holpop* meant "man-who-sits-at-the-head-of-the-mat." He was also in charge of the sacred drums and other musical instruments.

The lowest in the scale of officials was a *tupil*, the man who saw that the orders of the governor were carried out. These people lived in the center of the city. Beyond came the houses of the common Indians.

All of the Maya cities (there were uncalculated hundreds) were built in the same manner. In the center of the city was a large plaza, in front of which stood the largest temple. This was surrounded by the houses of priests and nobles. A few ordinary Mayas also lived within Tulum, but most did not. There was a reason for this, and the reason was lack of water.

Although it rains heavily in Yucatán, there are no rivers. When it rains, the water sinks into the thin soil rapidly and trickles down through porous limestone rock to form underground rivers below the surface. Ah Tok often found fossil sea shells in the rocks near Tulum, for limestone is formed from the shells of mollusks such as the scallop, triton, and nautilus, which for millions and millions of years have collected at the bottom of the ocean. Sometime in eons past, there had been an upheaval of this compressed lime matter from the ocean floor, and when thrust up, it became land which in time was covered with thin soil. Because limestone rock is soft, the earth here and there caved in, and natural wells bubbled up from the underground rivers under the rock. These were the *cenotes*, the one source of water around which the Mayas fashioned their cities.

Tulum had only one *cenote*, and for this reason it never grew into a larger city. The well lay close to the northeast sally port of Tulum, right at the gate, and was enclosed by a temple, which was called the Cenote House. Every evening the women came to this underground reservoir to draw their water. One of Ah Tok's earliest memories was his going to this well with his mother, who balanced a great water jug on her head at the same time, that she carried him on her hip. In the fashion of all Maya women, his mother always went bare-foot and wore a *kub,* a chemiselike dress made from a single piece of beautifully woven cloth with openings for the arms and head. All Maya women had pierced earlobes so they could wear earrings; these were of jade or gold. Their hair was their pride, though. This was worn in braids which were then twisted into coils decorated with gaily colored ribbons and placed on top of the head. At Tulum the water of the *cenote* was thirty feet below the surface, and the women had to walk down stone steps to reach it. While filling their jugs they gossiped and chatted, and the children splashed in the cool sweet water.

Mayas seldom drank pure water, however. They preferred it mixed with ground corn, which gave it a milky white color; in this form it was called *posole.*

Although Ah Tok's house, the Nā, was of simple, easy construction, it was in its way, quite beautiful. Its style was very ancient. It seems that the ordinary Mayas always built their houses of adobe and reeds worked in the same fashion.

When a house was to be built, various members of the clan helped. First they built a platform made of rock and adobe. Then large, upright tree trunks were set on top of the platform. A Nā was made so that it was rounded at both ends, and in the center was a single doorway—"the mouth of the house." The main roofpost in the middle of the house was called "the leg of the house"; after the roof purlins had been laid, it was called "the road of the rat," because rats lived in the palm-leaf roofing and used it as their principal roadway.

Serving as a framework for the adobe, were long, slender and pliable reeds, which the builders wove back and forth on the body of the house as if they were making a basket.

The adobe, itself, was made in the following way. A hole was filled with a mixture of mud and water, which was allowed to rest for some days, to "ferment." Then it was kneaded; the boys in the family actually jumped around in the mixture, churning the gray mud until their bodies were covered with it. After being worked in this way it then became adobe. The men picked it up in handfuls and slapped it on the wickerwork until the house was thickly plastered with adobe inside and out. Then the sharply pitched roof was thatched with palm leaves. Since houses were objects of great pride among the Mayas, they were painted in bright colors: red, orange, yellow, or blue. Mayas did not use doors; not even the great houses of the nobles had a door. Nevertheless, one never entered the house of another without permission. It was not done. Some Mayas hung a woven drapery across the door; Ah Tok's house, like others, had only a string to which were attached a number of copper bells for attracting notice.

A Maya house was divided into two sections. In one section was the kitchen. Since the Maya mother was her own baker, she had to make the unsalted, unleavened corncakes which were so popular throughout all Mexico and Yucatán. First she boiled dried corn in limewater to soften the grains. Then she washed it and ground it into a mush on a stone quern, or hand mill. This grinding stone stood next to the stove where stones were placed to hold pots. On top of the stove was a baking griddle to bake the corncakes. The kitchen utensils hung on the walls.

In one corner, in a niche in the wall, was set a clay idol of the moon goddess Ixchel, who was also the goddess of weaving.

Under this niche was a wall peg to which one end of the loom was attached. At night, or during the day when there was no other work, the women wove cotton cloth, for women did all the weaving. It was done on a back-strap loom, a simple device so-named because the weaver tightened the threads in the cloth by pulling the loom tight by means of a strap around her back.

The second section of the house contained the sleeping quarters. Beds were made of saplings tied together and placed on four forked sticks. Other peoples to the south used hammocks, but the Mayas liked beds better. Clothes, headdresses, and weapons were hung on the wall. A finely woven rush-basket held their more precious things: festive clothes and jade, turquoise, and feather headdresses if they had them.

On wooden pegs hung spears, bow and arrows, and wooden shields. All able-bodied Mayas were warriors; in fact, they were both warriors and farmers. When war was upon them, they dropped what they were doing, picked up spear and shield, and left for battle. Ah Tok was far too young for all this, of course, but he spent every spare moment learning to throw the spear and shoot with bow and arrow.

But now, in February, there was no time for play. March was the tribute month, and the entire household was busy working at their things for tribute. Every six months all those who were ruled by Tulum paid their tax. They could not pay taxes in money, since they had none. But they often used cacao beans, from which chocolate is made, as money. Chocolate was a Maya passion. Cacao beans, larger than peanuts, grew on thick-trunked trees in the hot, humid zone along riverbanks. It was a great event in the life of Ah Tok and his brothers whenever they were allowed to have chocolate. Their mother toasted the bean, crushed it into a powder, and to this added hot water, honey, and vanilla. Because every Maya desired chocolate, it took the place of money. A pumpkin was worth four cacao beans, a rabbit, ten . . . A Maya could buy a slave for a hundred cacao beans.

The *batab* was the tax collector as well as the governor of Tulum. Every household had to provide a piece of woven cotton cloth which had to be brought to the temple. As an individual, each citizen—with the exception of the leaders, who were not taxed—paid his taxes in the product with which he traded. Beekeepers brought honey and wax; a fisherman might be called upon to provide dried fish. Once all of the tax contributions were collected, the *batab* then gave part to the merchants, who used it to trade in distant lands for gold, bright feathers, or other things needed to decorate the temples or to clothe the officials.

The second part of the people's tax was in the form of work-service. When the farmer (almost all Mayas were farmers) had sowed his crops and had some leisure, he gave time to the state of Tulum. The chieftains' houses were built by Mayas working under an architect's ·direction as part of their work-service.

Masons cut blocks of limestone while others made limestone cement. Carpenters made the great wooden beams which held up the stone roof. Later, the stone was covered with a lime plaster, and on this a sculptor molded figures of the gods in stucco. It was finally painted.

For this reason, Mayan farmers were also craftsmen. They gave their time, and together, as a community effort, they built their cities. In this way, they built the great white *sacbe* roads; in this way, the trees were cut; and stone-built cities were thus raised in the jungle's stead.

The Mayas had done this for hundreds of katuns (a *katun* is approximately twenty years). Perhaps many of them thought they would go on forever. But there had been many disputes and many wars among them, and there were now many cities, each with its own governor. There was no Maya capital, no head of state, no king. Each tribal state refused to be ruled by any other. When disaster fell upon them, when it did not rain and their crops burned from the hot sun and there was famine, cities often did not co-operate with each other.

And to make matters worse in these years, out in the ocean-sea, coming from somewhere unknown, were bearded men coming into their lands. . . .

THE PROPHECY OF 8 AHAU

THE BEATING of the drums awakened Ah Tok. These drums had a different sound from those used by the guards. This sound came from the *tunkul,* a large upright drum that was as tall as Ah Tok. When beaten with rubber-tipped beaters the sound could be heard for miles away.

When he got there, the plaza was filled with all the inhabitants of Tulum. Those who lived outside the walls had also come in. It was still dark, and stars filled the heavens. On a flat platform in front of the main temple a priest was chanting, and the drummer kept the beat. The priest was reciting the prophecy of 8 Ahau, from the folded page in the Maya book of prophecies. On that day in earlier times many dire things had happened. Now they were at that day again and—once more—the large ships of the "bearded ones" had been seen. The priests exhorted all present to search their lives. He wanted them to give themselves to prayer. The *batab* was present, too, dressed in a jaguar skin and golden sandals. A large headdress of green quetzal feathers cascaded down his back. In his hand he held a spear, which he shook at the sea.

That day, men did not go to work in their fields. Instead, they sat in the close corners of their houses and talked of what this meant to them. The wise elders thought that these strange men must be the followers of Kukulkan. Did he not say when he sailed away that he would one day return?

Times had been troubled when Kukulkan came into Maya-land many centuries before. He had brought peace and unity. The Mayas who had been fighting among themselves then were brought together under one ruler and one capital. Now troubled times were once more on them, and Kukulkan was returning. As for the beards . . . the gods had a way of changing their appearance. So the men argued.

The younger boys, who were not admitted to the discussions, tried to overhear what was being said; but what they heard only left them puzzled. They knew something about their history, of course, for boys went to a sort of school maintained by each clan of the same family name. There, an old man who could no longer work in the fields and who knew the old stories would relate events of the past. Sometimes a warrior would come and show the boys how to use their weapons—how to set a flint arrowhead into its shaft, and how to pull a bow and make the arrow fly. They also learned to use the atlatl, a small wooden device that fitted into the hand and was shaped to carry the shaft of a spear. Using this, a greater force could be put into the thrust of a spear.

Often the boys fought mock battles under the eyes of their

warrior-teacher. Each was armed with a *chimaz,* a round shield made of tapir- or manatee-hide. Even though it was very light in weight, it was as tough as the hardest wood. The heavy, wide swords were made of wood, but when they went into battle, soldiers set obsidian into the sides of the swords, making them as sharp as knives. Ah Tok had once seen his father cut off the head of a deer with a single swish of the sword.

The war games and the tales related by the old men of the clan taught something of their people's past. But most of what they knew they learned from their parents and the other members of the family. Learning was by doing. As soon as a Maya child could walk, he began to do as his parents did, sharing in the work of the house. If the child was a girl, she learned to spin cotton into a ball of yarn, and helped her mother to dye it, thus learning which plants gave a red color, which berries, a yellow. She began to weave just as soon as her fingers could hold the bobbins of the loom.

Sons were taught by their fathers. First, about farming, then about hunting, and if they lived near the sea, as Ah Tok did, they were taught how to fish and hunt the great manatee and how to paddle a canoe. Since everyone built his own house, boys could learn about building by helping.

It is also significant that all Maya men were craftsmen. Some made good bows and arrows; others wove baskets from the osiers that grew in the jungles. Many worked in jade, the green stone which all Mayas wanted to wear on their persons, some of them fashioning it into the most precious jewels.

Ah Tok's father was a maker of blowguns. He knew how to select the branch of the best tree for his purpose—very hard outside, but with soft pith inside. He bored out the pith with a sharp pronged vine until it was hollow. Then he traced the size of the blowgun's bore on a sea shell and bored a hole this size in it with his tools. He then made clay pellets that were just big enough to pass through the hole in the sea shell. When the pellets were the exact size of the original bore in the blowgun, they were baked until they were as hard as rocks. These pellets, placed in the mouthpiece of a blowgun and ejected by a hard, sharp puff, could kill small birds instantly. Ah Tok re-

membered how he had once been hit on the head with a pellet and had carried his bump for several days.

Children also learned by listening. The Mayas had hundreds of chants and songs, which they sang to the beat of the drum or the chirp of the flute. These songs were histories and told of the early days. They sang of the wars the Mayas had fought, of the gods who had done them good or evil, of their days of happiness and of sorrow.

Ah Tok's grandfather, Ah Kuat, was a *chac,* a highly respected official. A *chac* helped the priests prepare their ceremonies and when there was to be human sacrifice, he helped to hold down the selected one. When Mayas wished to marry, a *chac* prepared the rituals.

Ah Kuat was as wise as a serpent, and in fact, his name meant "serpent." He had lived long and seen many things. Most important of all, he knew how to read and write the Maya writing. In a small stone house, close to the Great Temple where the priests lived, was a room in which the sacred books were kept. Ah Kuat was in charge of these books, and thus knew much about Maya history. The ever curious Ah Tok often sought information from his learned grandfather.

What then had the priest meant that morning when he had said: "This is the prophecy of 8 Ahau"? And what had this to do with all that was happening, and what had it to do with the "bearded ones"?

The old man, his hands shaking with the age that was upon him, slowly opened the book. Although he painted his face over the tattoo marks which had been put there when he was a young warrior, the only ornament he wore was a jade necklace. Like all Mayas, he had had his earlobes perforated when he was a young boy, and he had continued enlarging the opening until a duck's egg could have passed through it. In other times he had worn large turquoise ornaments in his ears, but now he thought no more about it. The skin of his earlobes hung down in folds like the wattles of a turkey.

The book he opened was painted on bark-paper. It came from the wild fig tree, or *copó*, a large tree with whitish bark and long branches that embraced other trees and crushed them to death. The Mayas called it a "tree killer." Ah Tok had often seen the paper made. The bark was cut at the top of the trunk and pulled free. A white sticky sap ran out of it just as the sap runs out of the sapodilla tree (from which chewing gum is made) when it is cut. The papermakers first soaked the bark in water to get rid of this sap. Then they beat the bark with a wooden beater into which ridges had been cut. Soon the fibers began to spread; within a few days a piece of bark originally two palms wide could be stretched by beating until it was six feet wide. It was beaten as thin as necessary and then cut into strips for books.

A Maya book was usually about eight inches high. Made of a single piece of paper sometimes as long as fifteen feet, it was then folded together like a screen. Each fold or leaf was called a *katun*. When the paper had been coated with lime to provide

a white surface, the priest was ready to write on it. It was in these books, Ah Tok knew, that the Mayas preserved their histories. The writing was difficult to understand, but the portraits of the gods were easy to recognize. Itzamna, a sky god, was usually pictured as sitting cross-legged. On his head was an elaborate headdress, and in his hand he held something like a light. He was a friend to man and the inventor of writing. The war god was painted in broad red-and-black stripes, just as warriors in Tulum now painted themselves. Each god had his own picture.

Then there was the writing, which were symbols of animals, birds, and other things in their environment, each having a special meaning. As for numbers, Ah Tok could only understand the simple ones: a dot (•) meant *one;* a bar (——) meant *five.* If an artist-priest wrote the number this way (≣) it meant *eighteen.* When he wanted to write *twenty,* he used a picture of a shell and a dot (⬩). Ah Tok was able to write these, but beyond this he could only wonder.

The old man read the page, his finger slowly following the signs and symbols:

> "This is the prophecy of 8 Ahau.
> This is what occurred at the death of Mayapán.
> Evil are the things which occur in this katun and on this date."

What did all this mean? In order to understand it, one had to know something of the past. It had begun a long, long time ago. . . .

It was a time which the books called *Mamón,* or "time of the grandmother." It was perhaps two thousand years ago. The Mayas had emigrated from the north, where Mexico now lies and where live the Aztecs, the tribe that call themselves Tenochas. Living on roots and berries, hunting deer and tapir, the Mayas slowly achieved their own way of living. It was in the Maya time of *Tzakol,* or "the builders," that they learned to build temples of stone and to fashion beautiful pottery.

It was also during this time that the Mayas learned to write. Their priests studied the stars. They knew when the planet Venus appeared and when it disappeared. They found out when the moon would be full and when a crescent. In time, they made a calendar. And with the newly invented writing, the priests began to record the history of the Mayas. Every time they completed a building they put up a time-marker. These were great stone slabs, similar to the ones in the center of Tulum, only larger. On them, sculptors carved the figure of the ruler of that time, and the dates which the priest gave them.

From 300 A. D. until 700 A. D. the Mayas built great cities. In the lands behind Yucatán where there are jungles and rivers, the Mayas built great cities. No one living now has seen them all, said Ah Kuat, and even their names are forgotten. But one day when he himself was young, when the Maya capital of Mayapán had fallen, he had fled with others to a great inland lake called Petén. Near-by they found an immense city, which was called Tikal. It was so large that Tulum would be lost if placed in its center. Pyramids were so high that they rose above the tallest trees, and, indeed, most of the buildings were overgrown with trees and vines. Only one small temple was not covered over, and it was here the priests from Petén went when they wanted to communicate with the old gods. The people of Petén told Ah Kuat that beyond this, in the jungles, there were many such old cities. All were of stone and all built, more or less, like the larger Maya cities in Yucatán.

The story continued. . . .

DAYS

IMIX · IK · AKBAL · KAN · CHICCHAN

CIMI · MANIK · LAMAT · MULUC · OC

CHUEN · EB · BEN · IX · MEN

CIB · CABAN · EZNAB · CAUAC · AHAU

MONTHS

POP · UO · ZIP · ZOTZ · TZEC

XUL · YAXKIN · MOL · CHEN · YAX

ZAC · CEH · MAC · KANKIN · MUAN

PAX · KAYAB · CUMHU · UAYEB

About 890 something terrible happened. Rain did not fall, crops dried up, people died by the thousands. All over the land the people left their cities in search of food, and many never returned. Tribes the Mayas had never seen before began to come down from Mexico where the drought was equally terrible. When this period was over, and the Mayas returned to the cities, great changes had taken place. The priests no longer carved stone time-markers, or "talking-stones"; instead, they began to put their histories into paper books, just like the one Ah Kuat now was reading.

Many of the coastal cities were as old as most of those in the jungles and the Mayas had always lived in them, but not in very great numbers.

Now, after that "something" happened, they began to come to Yucatán in great multitudes. Older cities, like the great Chichén Itzá, were reoccupied. The temples were made larger; the ball court was enlarged. All along the coast there was a quickening of life.

In the year 987, on November 27, to be exact, the Toltecs arrived. The old man's fingers traced the pictures, the symbols, and the date 4 Ahau 13 Cumhu.

The Toltecs came from the high mountains of Mexico and, like the Mayas, they were a very ancient people. They were great builders and famous artists. When anyone of another tribe excelled at painting or sculpture he was called a "Toltec." Toltecs were also warriors, and they fought wars with all the tribes about them. Then one day their turn came. During a war their capital was destroyed, and the Toltecs were forced to leave. They moved north of their old capital and built the city of Tula. And it was from this city that, hundreds of years later, a clan called the Itzás wandered off into exile toward Yucatán, where their destiny became linked with that of the Maya. It took the Toltecs two hundred years to build Tula. They had a great leader, Quetzalcoatl, or the Plumed Serpent. He was called this because his symbol was the open jaw of a snake with the golden-green plumes of the quetzal bird.

The old myths are not clear about whether the Plumed Serpent was a god before he became a man, or whether he was a man before he became a god. But in Tula, the Plumed Serpent was a man, a ruler of the city-state. He was much loved by some of the people, but by others he was not loved at all. A civil war began between them. The Plumed Serpent lost and was forced to leave. Thousands of his Toltec followers went with him. After much wandering they came down to a place along the seacoast which was close to the land of the Mayas.

This place, Xicalango, was set back from a large lagoon in a region known as "the land-where-the-language-changes." To the south people spoke Maya, and to the north people spoke

Toltec invaders

the Aztec language. Xicalango was the great trading center to which Indians from all Mexico came to trade the things they made for Maya products. No wars were permitted here.

It was in this region that the Plumed Serpent and the people he had brought with him learned the Maya language and, as they had no home of their own, they began to occupy the old cities that the Mayas had abandoned years before. So in 987 they came to Chichén Itzá, an old Maya city that had first been built in 452, and then deserted.

The Plumed Serpent built the very beautiful temples which Ah Tok will be able to see when he goes there. On the great pyramid he had his own symbol placed, and he built the large ball court, the greatest anyone had ever seen. And most of all, he brought unity to the Mayas. Before he had come there was much strife. But he said that since all were brothers, spoke the same language, wore the same clothes, worshiped the same gods, why did they have to make war against one another? Accepting this philosophy, the Mayas proclaimed him both ruler and god. They called him Kukulkan, the Maya name for Plumed Serpent.

Kukulkan decided that the Mayas should have a capital. Wisely realizing that each of the many cities wanted such an honor for themselves, and knowing that this would begin warfare among the cities again, Kukulkan built a new city. It was located no farther than a day's travel on foot from Chichén Itzá.

First they built a very broad stone wall, three times as large as the one that surrounds Tulum. It had only two narrow gates. Within that wall they built a city, which was named Mayapán, or Flag of the Mayas. It was a miniature of Chichén Itzá with

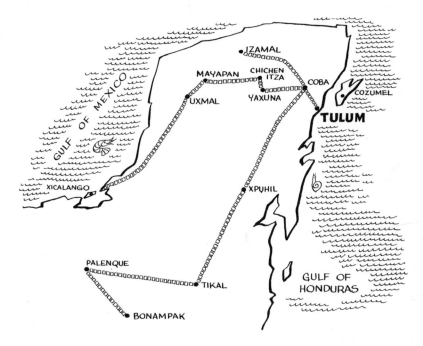

temples, pyramids, and ball courts. Every noble had to have a house in the city and live there many months of the year. Peace and plenty now filled the land.

One day Kukulkan left the Mayas. He said he wanted to return to his home in Mexico. The people showed much sorrow, but they could not stay him. He left by a great seagoing canoe from a place on the shore now called Champotón, and in his memory the people built a fine building.

It is written that he left the region in katun 2 Ahau—June 23, 1017—promising that he would one day return. So remembering this, they believe that the new people who come out of the sea now, the "bearded ones," are Kukulkan. So the old man continued going over the talking-book and spoke:

"Mayapán was a great city for more than four hundred years. During this time there were no wars between the Mayas. We knew trade and peace. I, Ah Kuat, was born within the walls of Mayapán, and I remember . . . We, our family, are descendants of those from Tula, whom they called 'Itzás.' But in Yucatán there were other great lords, the Cocoms. They talked very big. They said that they and not the Itzás were the 'natural lords' of Yucatán.

"One day one of them went to this Xicalango, the land-where-the-language-changes. There he hired Mexican warriors to aid him in conquering all Yucatán for his family alone. And so he did. These warriors always went about with the Cocoms, who also claimed descent from the Plumed Serpent God, and soon there was discord among us. All of the Cocoms were living at Mayapán . . . all except one who was away on a trading expedition to get cacao beans. Then one night . . . the chiefs of the other tribes who hated the Cocoms came silently into the city and . . . at the blast from a conch shell they sprang on all of their people. Every Cocom was killed; all of the Mexican hired warriors were killed; even some of our own people were killed by mistake. I was a little boy then on that night of 1441. But I remember. . . . The walls were overthrown, the houses ruined. Our idols broken . . .

"After that Mayapán was a broken city. My father gathered up as many of the sacred books that we could find and left for Tulum. Other Itzá-Mayas escaped to the great Petén lake deep in the jungle, five days' walk from here. After the fall of Mayapán the nobles again began their wars, one city against another. We were no longer united. We fight amongst ourselves. That is what the prophecy means." And Ah Kuat repeated it:

"This is the prophecy of 8 Ahau.
This is what occurred at the death of Mayapán.
Evil are the things which occur in this katun and on this date."

Ah Kuat continued: "When the great calendar, which turns like a wheel, repeats the same date on which evil occurred . . . terrible things will happen again. Like the time of the hurricane. The prophecy was repeated by the priests, but the people took no heed. That night a great wind arose. It blew in from the sea. It tore up trees by their roots, and it blew down the houses, overturning them and causing them to take fire. Great splinters from trees flew in the air, killing many people. The wind lasted for a day and a night. When at last it had blown itself away, the whole land had changed. The forest was cut off at the top as if one of the gods had cut it with a gigantic pair of scissors. Then followed the pestilence. And again our people died by the thousands. Much was lost. Much was changed—even the name of the land. At one time, it had been called the Land of the Turkey and the Deer. . . .

"Now we, the Mayas, are again disunited. And there is more disaster ahead for us. The talking-book says so. Time upon time out on the ocean-sea come large ships. They are not our ships. They are sailed by men with blue eyes and large beards. Our eyes are black, and we have no beards. Some of the bearded men, whoever they are, are already among us.

"Rónimo is one of them. He is here, even though he is a slave. He is one of the 'bearded ones.'"

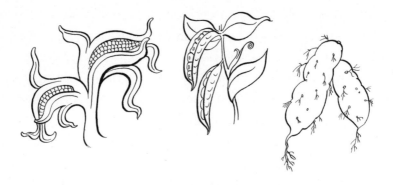

WITH THE EARTH GODS

THE MONTH of Mol was the last of the harvest months, and since there was a corn surplus, it was one of the tribute months.

It was now very hot, as it is in all tropic lands in the month of March. The corn, which had ripened, had been turned down on the stalks to dry and also to prevent the birds from eating it.

The cornfields of Tulum lay toward the west. Beyond the great wall of Tulum, the forest was filled with palm trees, tall cedars, and low bushes. It was in this forest that the Mayas prepared their fields.

Ah Tok and his brothers went with their father along with everyone else who was old enough to work in the fields. First they cut down the forest. This was man's work. And every man of the same clan helped one another. Trees had to be cut with a *bat,* or stone ax, for the Mayas had no metal. When Ah Tok tried to cut a tree with a small copper ax that he had traded with another boy—whose father had brought it from Panamá —the hard tree turned the metal ax's edge like wax. Although stone axes were hard and sharp, the Indian still had to stop occasionally and chip the ax to bring it to a sharper point. So

44

the trees were felled. Then in the dry season they were burned. The logs that did not burn were dragged away to make a fence to keep the deer and the tapirs from eating the young plants. Then with a fire-hardened stick the earth was turned and plowed. All worked at this, the women as well as the men. Afterward, the land was divided.

The land belonged to the clans and the tribe. It belonged to all. Every planting year the *batab* came to measure the land. While he stood there, very proud in his feather headdress, the men measured, using a tape measure twenty feet long. Each *col*, or cornfield, was to be twenty measures of the tape in length and twenty measures of the tape in width (thus, four hundred feet square). If a man had a large family, he was given more *cols;* if the family was small, he was allotted fewer. Larger families had as many as ten fields.

Between June and August it rained heavily, and the ground was soft and ready for planting. The priest then came to the fields to read from his almanac. There, in the old books, it told when the time was good to plant and when there were luck-filled days.

"This is 9 Caban. It is a good time; it is a lucky time. Heavy rains will fall; it is a good time for planting everything."

Then all the people would come together to help plant each other's fields. None would leave the forest until all the corn-fields had been planted. When the corn grew to be knee-high, the Mayas planted beans next to each stalk. These black beans, which they called *bul*, would then entwine around the growing corn plant. In other fields, they planted the pale sweet potato and the cassava, which is also a starchy vegetable. Around the edges of the field on the burned logs, they grew chayotes and other fruit-yielding vines.

The life of the Maya centered around the cornfield. If an Indian worked hard, he would only have to spend one hundred days during the year as a farmer. His fields would give him enough corn to feed his family, and he would have much left over to trade for other things that he needed. It was this leisure time that the cultivation of corn gave him which allowed him to give time to his city. With that time he worked with all others to build the temples and the other buildings which made the Maya cities the most famous of the land.

For as long as Ah Tok could remember, he went to the cornfields. When he was small, his parents tied him to his cradle, placing it in the shade, while they all worked in the fields. When he was four years old, he went to play in the cornfield, and by the time he was eight, he began to help. Now, at thirteen, he did the work of a man.

And he ate like a man; that is, he was given just as much

food as an adult. The first meal of the day consisted of *posole,* the thick ball of corn paste which was stirred into a gourd of water. On the way to the fields and jungles they carried some corncakes, beans, or a piece of deermeat or turkey perhaps. A narrow-necked gourd held their water. This was all they had to eat during the day, unless Ah Tok was fortunate enough to find a nest of honeybees. At nighttime they would eat their warm meal.

For Ah Tok, the jungle was a friendly place. During midday, when it was very hot and the cicadas raised their voices to such a din that one could not hear himself talk, he liked to wander off alone with his blowgun. There were always so many birds. The quail, as brown as dead leaves, ran along the ground; the red-headed woodpecker did not seem to care how much racket it made pecking at the dead wood. The jays, as blue as the color used by the Mayas to paint their houses, were always about. Noisy and unafraid, they moved in flocks, as many as a hundred at a single time.

The wild turkey was the one Ah Tok most liked to hunt. Its

flesh was good eating, but best were its feathers, which warriors used for headdresses. Other big jungle birds included the yellow-crested *cambul,* as large as a turkey, with a black hooked beak and yellow head.

A great variety of parrots were hunted for their feathers. Ah Tok never tried to kill such a bird unless it was needed for food. That is why he used his blowgun. Aiming at the bird's body, he gave a sharp puff and the clay pellet stunned it. When it fell to the ground, he would only pluck out a few feathers and then let the bird fly away again.

The dry Yucatán jungles were full of animals. There were many deer. So many, in fact, that the land had been called the Land of the Turkey and the Deer. The deer were killed with bow and arrow and sometimes with a spear, but since Ah Tok was not yet strong enough to bend back the big bow, he could only wish for the day he would be old enough to use a hunter's weapons.

Like all Indians, he had respect for animals. He believed that they, too, had souls. When Ah Tok's father was about to kill a deer, he said a little prayer: "O god of the animals, I have need." Then he would release the arrow. When the animal had been skinned and prepared, he was careful to clean the skull with the antlers. These he placed in the kitchen near the fire as a form of respect. The Mayas believed that if they did not do this, the dead animal would communicate any disrespect to all of its kind and as the result none of these animals would in the future allow themselves to be killed.

The tapir, called *tzimín,* was the largest animal in the jungle. It had a thick body, rather short legs, and a great head. It was a timid beast, eating only grass that grew around the small lakes which appeared during the rainy seasons. But the tapir was very strong, and it could not be killed with a bow and

arrow. If a Maya killed one, he was considered a brave man, for he had had to get close enough to the animal to spear its hard, tough flesh. It was so seldom that this was accomplished, that fathers left the skins to their sons as heirlooms.

The dry ground of the jungle was mixed with rocks and vines. Here there lived a number of smaller animals. There were foxes and opossums and the *zub,* an armadillo which when newly born looked like a small pig. There were large rabbits which were good-tasting, and there was a little agouti, sad by nature, which went out only at night and lived in small caves during the day. Ah Tok used to set a trap for this; they were good eating.

The funniest animal was the *chic,* a coati belonging to the raccoon family which went along in large herds. It had short legs, a long furry body, a ringed tail which it kept high in the air, and a very long flexible nose. All Mayas were very fond of them; in fact, they often kept a tame one at home. The women took good care of them, feeding them, bathing them, and even removing their lice.

Lions also came to the jungle to feed on the deer and the smaller brockets, those deer with short, unbranched horns. But most often lions stayed in the higher mountains, venturing down to hunt in Yucatán only when very hungry. The jaguar was feared by everyone. Only the bravest of the brave dared to kill it. But some Indians learned how to make a jaguar trap, and in this way they obtained the skins which the war chiefs made into cloaks.

When Ah Tok returned to the cornfield after his midday visit to the jungle, the men were already packing the corn. He joined them, placing ears of corn into large woven bags. Two Indians held up the bags while another slipped a rope around both the bag and the carrier's forehead. The Indians could carry ninety pounds all day long if they had to. The people themselves were their own beasts of burden. Ah Tok was a carrier too, but he could only carry thirty pounds. Forming a long line, the carriers followed the trail through the jungle back toward Tulum.

Immense cedars rose up, on the way, some of them as wide as six feet in diameter, and as high as a hundred feet. As they were passing through the cedar forest they came upon some slaves who were taking a newly made canoe to Tulum. The wooden shell—more than forty feet long and four feet wide— had been dug out until it was only an inch thick. It took much skill to make a fine canoe. First, the canoemaker had had to chop out several holes in the tree trunk. He built a fire in these holes so that when the fire died out, he could easily scrape out the burned part and build another fire. By doing this, time and time again, the canoe was eventually hollowed out.

The slaves, dirty and naked, continued to pull the canoe through the dry jungle. At the bow they had fastened two long ropes made of the spiny-leafed henequen plant. When the pads

of these century plants were dried and combed, they yielded long, tough fibers, which were then twisted together to form rope cables. Ah Tok had seen a henequen cable as thick as his wrist. Maya architects used them to raise or pull large stone monuments into place.

While twenty slaves were tightly gripping the ropes others were placing rollers under the canoe, so that it could be pulled. As soon as one roller was free, a slave picked it up, ran ahead, and replaced it in front of the bow of the canoe.

The rollers were made of hard *zapote,* or sapodilla, wood, and there were many such trees in the jungle. Ah Tok and his friends left their corn behind and searched for them. When they found a *zapote,* or "chewing-gum tree," they made deep gashes into the trunk. At once, a sort of milky juice gushed out, and it was not long before this substance became sticky. The boys gathered up this chicle, or *itz,* as they called it, made it into a wad which they stuck in their mouths, and then, chewing merrily, they went back to their packs.

The canoe was now in front of them, and as there was but one small trail, they slowed their pace to follow that of the canoe carriers. The big dugouts made in Tulum were famous throughout the land. Many Maya chieftains came there to trade for them. These then sailed all along the coast, far south, more than a thousand miles to Panamá! A member of Ah Tok's family had once gone along on one of these expeditions. It was the time when they had first met the "bearded ones." When he returned to Tulum he told his story over and over again.

It was like this. In the year recorded in the talking-books as 3 Ahau 2 Yax—the year 1502—a man from Tulum called Ah Cuy, or the Owl, was taking a new canoe to the south. He went to Omoa, in Honduras, where the Mayas had a trading colony. The fat chieftain there was organizing a trading trip to Guanaja Island, which was fifteen miles out to sea.

Ah Cuy went with them. When they arrived, they were surprised to see four ships, built like houses floating on water, at anchor there. They had never seen anything like it before. The men were clothed in a very strange manner, and they all wore beards. The man who seemed to be the chief had red hair and blue eyes.

None of the Indians could understand a word these strange men said. But they appeared to be friendly, and by means of hand signals, they asked for manta cloth, giving in return beads that looked like jade. The strangers also signaled a request for one of the Indians to go with them to the south to Panamá and act as an interpreter. Jimbe, one of the men in Ah Cuy's canoe, who knew some of these languages, agreed to go. They never saw Jimbe again.

Ah Cuy—as wise as his name, the Owl, would indicate— noticed that as the strangers talked, one man kept writing in something that looked like a Maya book. Ah Cuy looked over his shoulder, but could not make out the signs. To him, the writing looked like the sort of tracks lizards leave when they run over sand. When Ah Cuy pointed to the writing, the man noticed that he had a certain symbol, or glyph, tattooed on his hand. It stood for his name, so Ah Cuy pointed to the symbol and then slapped his chest, trying to indicate that he and the symbol on his hand were one and the same, and thus his name was the same "Ah Cuy," which he then pronounced. The "bearded one" understood. So then by the same gestures, Ah Cuy asked the name of their chieftain, that man with the red beard and the blue eyes. But Ah Cuy could not understand the answer. Then he had the idea of taking out a piece of bark-paper, which he gave to the man so that he could use the "talking-ink." On it, the man wrote his name: *Cristóbal Colón.*

Ah Cuy still kept this weathered piece of bark-paper among his treasures, next to a piece of tapir skin and the gold face-mask he had traded for in Honduras. Whenever he drank too much *balche,* the fermented honey which the Mayas made on their festive days, he would bring the bark-paper out. And once again he would tell the story.

These were the first "bearded ones" who had been seen. Ah Tok thought a good deal about it as he walked behind the canoe. It was only when they reached the clearing near the west gate of Tulum that Ah Tok first saw *him.* Among the slaves who were dragging the canoe was a man whose face Ah Tok had first thought was painted black. This seemed strange to him, because only honorable men were allowed to paint themselves. Then Ah Tok realized that although this strange slave's head was cropped like all the rest, he had a full beard.

Ah Tok stared so much that his father gestured to him to close his mouth. "The man you stare at," said his father, "is Rónimo. He is one of the 'bearded ones.'"

THE "BEARDED ONES"

THE *batab* had ordered it.

Every Maya was to stop what he was doing and work on the roads. Those who did not hear the order direct, heard it from the lips of Ah Tok's father, the *tupil*. For it was his duty to see that the orders were obeyed. The roads must be repaired.

The bearded strangers had been seen again. The *batab* wanted everything put into a state of defense, and most important were the roads. Tulum had a treaty with other cities in the interior, whose warriors would come to help Tulum if the enemy were to land on her shores. So the roads must be repaired.

North of Tulum, at a distance of only a two-hour walk over the road, was the city of Xelha. It was smaller than Tulum, but it also had a wall about it. In its way, it too was an important city, because the main Maya roads led to it. The road from Xelha led into the interior.

54

A short distance from Xelha was the city of Cobá. Further along, about seventy miles west, were other Maya cities. Then the road turned north, and from here led to the greatest city of Yucatán—Chichén Itzá. From there roads went out in all directions.

It was a very upsetting time. The people were afraid of what they had heard. Twice in recent years these strange people had landed on their shores, and both times the Mayas had attacked them and sent them scurrying to their ships.

Now a famous priest had come to the coast. He wore a white bark-cloth raiment, and his face was scarred with tattoo marks. The lower part of his ear hung as ribbons, since he had cut his own ear to draw blood for sacrifice so many times before. He had put his own blood on idols of the gods so that they would reveal the future to him. His title was: He-who-has-the-duty-of-giving-the-answer-of-the-gods. After consulting his sacred picture books and the liver of a turkey as well as the wing of a dead vulture, the oracle had said:

"We will be overrun by another people who preach a god who has the power of a tree."

There were few who knew what this meant. But the *batab* of Tulum, clothed in a jaguar skin and a fine helmet of green feathers, strode back and forth. He shouted that whoever the strangers were, they would have to fight to take the Mayas' lands from them.

So the roads had to be repaired, and for days the Indians had been gathering conch shells. The Maya fishermen dived for these enormous shellfish, bringing thousands to the surface each day. As large as a man's head, they moved very slowly in the sea, looking much like gigantic snails. After the Indians had removed the animal they sometimes cleaned the inside of the shell and then made a tiny hole at the smaller end of it. It had lips like those of a trumpet and it sounded like one. Such shells were used at religious feasts, and were also used by the guards at Tulum to give signals. When people played music, the conch was always used to give deep sound.

In addition, conch was also used to make cement. Great piles of conch shells now lay gathered on the beach. Other Indians had brought wood, which they piled around the shells and then set on fire. After the fire had burned down, it left a huge mound of shell powder. Mixed with very light sand, the powder became a durable white cement.

Now the cement was scooped into cotton bags which were put on the backs of slaves, who then moved off toward the inner road. It was tiresome work and the heat was unbearable. At midday the sun was so hot that even the lizards looked for shade in which to hide. The Indians sat resting in the shade of trees that overhung the beach, and there they drank *posole.*

Apart from the others sat a tired-looking bearded man. After resting for a few minutes with his back against a tree, he took a small worn book from his net bag. Ah Tok knew this man was Rónimo, and he wanted to talk to him. He wanted to find out directly from him about all his people.

Rónimo answered him in the Maya language. Anyone could have sensed that it was not his real language. Yet he spoke well. When he saw that Ah Tok was sincere, he told him his story.

His name was not Rónimo, it was Gerónimo, Gerónimo de Aguilar. As the boy could not understand it, Gerónimo showed him a page in his book. On the first page was written: *Gerónimo de Aguilar.* He explained that he had studied for the priesthood in Spain. But he was also interested in the sea, so he became a sailor and went to the New World. One day he sailed from

Panamá toward Cuba. This was the island—he pointed in a northerly direction—where the Carib Indians live. On the tenth day at sea, their ship ran on the rocks near Jamaica. The ship began to sink, and those who could, got into their small lifeboat, but they had no water, no food, no sails.

The little boat drifted for days. When the first sailors died they were thrown overboard. But soon the sharks and the barracudas began to follow the boat day and night. After that they kept the dead with them. On the thirteenth day they drifted to a large island. They were so weak that they hardly had the strength to paddle their lifeboat ashore. As soon as they set foot on the shore, Maya Indians ran down to the water and surrounded them.

With their arms tied behind them, the sailors were marched to a sort of cage. Those who were too weak to walk, were carried on litters resembling fish nets. A pole was merely passed between the net. No one among the ten remaining Spaniards knew the Maya language. They did not know that they had drifted to Cozumel, a sacred Maya island. The next morning Captain Valdivia was sacrificed. He was laid upon a carved stone, and his arms and legs were held tightly down by four old men, who were called *chacs*. A priest held up a flint knife and pulled it sharply across the victim's chest. Then the priest pushed in his hand, grasped the heart which was still beating, and wrenched it out.

Gerónimo was very weak, and there was so little water left in his body after all the exposure in the open boat that he could not even shed tears. The next day four more of his friends, who had been painted with blue paint, the color of sacrifice, were killed. Three others died before they could be offered to the Maya gods. The only ones now left were he and another crew member, Gonzalo the Mariner. Why hadn't they been sacrificed? Rónimo believed that they were being saved for another day. They were given food and drink; in fact, they were being fattened.

Then a great chieftain arrived at Cozumel.

This man, Ah Kin Cutz, wanted to take the two Spaniards as slaves. So they went back with Ah Kin Cutz to Tulum. At first, Gerónimo was a household slave, but then as he learned the Maya language he was able to tell his master about himself and his fellow Spaniards. All that Gerónimo told him about the bearded men interested the Maya, but it also frightened him.

One day as Gerónimo watched the Indian archers practicing—they were using an animal tied to a tree as target—Ah Kin Cutz came up behind him.

"Rónimo," he said, for he could not pronounce the Spaniard's full name, "what do you think of those archers? See how accurate they are. For he who aims at the eye, hits the eye; and he who aims at the mouth, hits the mouth. Do you think that if you were placed there in the animal's stead, they would miss you?"

Rónimo thought that the time had come for his sacrifice, but he answered, "My lord, I am your slave. And you can do what you wish with me. But you are too good and too wise to lose a slave like me who will serve you in whatsoever you command."

After this, Gerónimo had his master's confidence. When a battle was to be fought between Tulum and another Maya city, his master, the *batab,* asked his advice. How should the battle be fought? Gerónimo, who had fought Indians before, knew their weakness in battle. He drew a plan on the hard floor, which impressed the *batab,* who then called in his war captain and explained to him how the battle would be fought. Days later it was fought as the slave Rónimo had suggested. And the battle was won.

The defeated Maya captain was furious. He sent word with his ambassadors that Gerónimo should be sacrificed at once, "for the gods were angry with the *batab* of Tulum because he had conquered his own kind with the aid of a man not belonging to their race or their religion."

After this, Gerónimo never tried to help the Mayas fight battles. But his friend Gonzalo, the other Spaniard whose life had also been spared so that he could serve an important Maya as a slave, continued to guide the Mayas in battle. Gonzalo had married a Maya woman, who bore his children, and had adopted Maya customs, such as piercing his ears. Now he was no longer a slave; he was an important war-captain, a *nacom.* He lived like a great Maya lord in Chetumal province, just south of Tulum.

Ah Tok heard all this story with great wonderment. Still the
bearded man seemed very sad after telling it. He had been
away from his own people so long that he had almost forgotten his mother tongue. He had tried to keep his memory green
by reading aloud from the very worn psalter he now held in his
hands. It was his only book, and he had thumbed it almost to
pieces. It contained psalms which were sung in the church in
which Gerónimo's religion was practiced. It was the only thing
that kept alive the memory of his other days. In it were the feast
days, the holidays of the church. He explained to Ah Tok that
by keeping track of these special days, and noting their passing,
he had been able to record the passage of time since he had
come among Ah Tok's people. According to Spanish time, he
had been captured in 1511, so it now must be 1515.

The question uppermost in Ah Tok's mind was whether or
not Rómino thought that the "bearded ones" would return.
Would they, as the prophecy said, return and conquer the
Mayas and make them their slaves?

The Spaniard did not answer this at once. He knew that
many of the Mayas wanted him to be sacrificed. He knew too
that only the aid of his master, the *batab* of Tulum, saved him.
Indians were always asking him questions to trap him, to make
him say something which they could later use against him.

Rónimo replied by saying that the Castillians—for such was
the name he used for the men the Maya called the "bearded
ones"—lived on all those islands of the land without. And with
a sweep of his arm he indicated all the islands of the sea: Cuba
and all the others. Not only did the Carib Indians live there,
but the white man lived there too. He built cities, and he sailed
the sea on large ships. And those outsiders knew that the Mayas
lived in Yucatán. It is true that the Castillians who had come

here had been defeated, but in Rónimo's home of Spain, far, far away, there were thousands upon thousands more of these white men. To help Ah Tok understand how many this number actually was, Rónimo wrote in Maya figures on the sand the number ten thousand.

Now Ah Tok could understand. In a far-away place, there were many thousands of bearded men who had learned of Mayaland. These men would come and continue to come until they had finally conquered all this land.

Was this the prophecy of 8 Ahau?

"SACBE," THE GREAT ROAD

IT WAS two years later before Ah Tok finally had his chance
to go to Chichén Itzá. The trip to the great city had been
promised to Ah Tok and his brothers for a long time. His father
had said that, as the sons of a *tupil,* they should know more of
the land about them. During his childhood, Ah Tok had heard
about the great Maya city, with its tall pyramids and its immense ball court—where men played the game of *pok-a-tok*
with rubber balls. He had heard of the market, rich with trade
goods. How he had longed to see it!

But for the last year, as his grandfather said, the Maya world
was not as it had been. There had been many wars among the
Maya cities; people were jealous of each other. This had upset
life considerably. For Tulum, which lived off the large amount
of trade that went south toward Panamá, now had little of it.
Wars had closed the roads. And worse still, the "bearded ones"
had come again.

The *batab* had been right to see that the *sacbe*-highways were in good repair. Because without them, warriors could not have moved easily over the rough land. Yucatán was covered with sharp limestone and thick dry jungles.

In March, 1517—in the Maya 3 Ahau 18 Mac—two big ships had come to the northern tip of Yucatán, where the Maya removed salt from the salt lagoons. Some of the men of Tulum had been filling their canoes when the ships appeared there. On instructions from their chieftain, ten large canoes, each carrying forty Indians, had gone out to meet the vessels. As all seemed friendly, the Indians even went on board, and were astounded by all they saw.

The Maya lord then invited the visitors ashore, saying "Come to visit our houses." But after the Castillians had landed and were on their way, the Maya warriors planned an ambush in the tall bush. At a signal, the Indians attacked and killed fifteen Castillians. The bearded men then blew off a weapon which the Mayas had never seen nor heard. It was like a hollow tree trunk. Out of its mouth came flame and a noise like thunder. Twenty Maya warriors immediately fell dead. The fight lasted for some time, and then the white men retreated into a Maya city, looting it of its idols and a small amount of gold. They carried off two Maya Indians as captives and fled to their ships.

So peace returned to the land. Ah Tok's family—the Chen family—took the long-promised trip to Chichén Itzá.

It was the sixth month of the Maya year, the month of Xul when people throughout Yucatán honored their great patron, Kukulkan. The roads were crowded, since it was a very important festival. The Chen family entered the main royal road beyond Xelha.

The great road was called *sacbe* because *sac* meant "white,"

and this was indeed a white road. Fifteen feet wide, it was built like a causeway raised above the surface of the ground. To mark the width, the builders had first made a straight wall of stones on both sides. Then the road was filled with loose limestone until it became level within the high wall. All this was then filled with coarse gravel. And on top the builders put a finely ground lime-cement which spread evenly over the road's surface when it was mixed with water. The *sacbe* was a wonderful thing. All the Indians who traveled over it, marveled at this straight causeway which went through the dark aisle of the forest, white as the wings of an egret.

This day the road was filled with people moving toward Chichén Itzá. All of them were carrying cargo on their backs

by means of a rope which was strapped around the forehead of their flattened heads. There were so many of them hurrying forward at a half-running trot that, to Ah Tok, they seemed very much like those leaf-cutting ants who hold the cut leaf over their heads as if it were a sunshade, as they move to their underground gardens.

The *sacbe* road was spaced with stone markers to indicate distance. Every five miles or so a small road would lead off the main one to villages that lay somewhere out in the low jungle. At other points along the road there were small shrines. These were raised to the god of the North Star and protector of travelers. Ah Tok had been shown how to burn copal incense at each shrine and to pray to this god to help the travelers reach the journey's end in peace.

Cobá was the first large city on the road. It lay about twenty miles back from the sea. There were so many roads going in all directions, that the Chen family had to ask a dweller of that city to make sure they were on the right one.

Cobá was very old. The time-markers set up in the main plaza showed that the earliest one had been set up in Spanish time 682. Some said Cobá was a sacred city because it was built around lakes which were never without water.

A wide road, *sacbe* number 3 (• •) moved directly into the main plaza. Ah Tok could see at once that Cobá had been built on a plan different from Tulum's. The main square was large, four hundred feet long, and almost as wide. The massive, solid main temples rose up one behind the other. Steps, which people climbed, began at the plaza. At Tulum, the buildings were smaller and separated one from another, but here at Cobá they were massed together and one led into another. A large part of the city faced the lakes, just as Tulum faced the ocean.

Visitors to Cobá could stay at the travelers' house. Every Maya city and village had such a place for those who had traveled the roads. At these houses firewood was piled up and ready for use, and dried corn was set aside so that the women could make corncakes. Since the Mayas were taught from childhood to be generous to each other, no one ever went hungry. In addition to this, travelers could also find places to sleep, and food for their use, by the side of the roads.

The large Chen clan, to which Ah Tok's family belonged, was scattered all over Yucatán. The Mayas believed that all people who had the same name were of the same blood, and immediately upon meeting another, a Maya would ask him his name. If they were of the same name, then they were of the same family and at once each was invited to stay at the other's house.

Ah Tok's grandfather, who was traveling with them, explained it to Ah Tok this way: "We always call our sons and daughters by the name of their father and their mother. Your father is a Chen, and your mother is a Chan, so your whole name is Ah Tok Nachan Chen. *Na* means, of course, 'the son of.'

"At Cobá there is a large Chen family. We do not know each other directly, but if we have the same name, we must be of the same family, the same clan, and the same blood. And this is the reason why Mayas say that those bearing the same name are all of one family or clan and we are treated as such."

The Chen family, all eight of them, were welcomed to a large house not too distant from the plaza. The house was built like theirs in Tulum, only larger, for it housed a larger family. The roof, however, was pitched at a sharper angle, because it rained more heavily in Cobá. The sleeping quarters were large and spacious, and since the customs of eating, in which the men ate apart from the women, were the same as in Tulum, the visitors felt at home.

The festival of *emku* was now in progress. At a house near-by, a court had been swept very clean, and fresh leaves had been spread over the ground. In the court stood a group of boys, all under twelve years of age. In another group were girls about the same age. The boys wore no clothing, and the girls merely wore a large sea shell, which was held about their waists by a thick cord.

The children stood within the magic square, which was enclosed by a rope. At each corner of the square sat a *chac* on a wooden stool, holding the rope in his hand. *Chacs* were old and honorable men of the city chosen for this ritual of *emku*.

Ah Tok remembered having gone through this ritual when he was twelve years of age. And at that time his own grandfather had been one of the *chacs* who had participated.

The magic square was made so that no evil spirits could pass over the rope and harm the children. The *chilan,* or priest, came forward. A man of noble bearing, he went about in a cloak of red-feather weaving, and on his head he wore a large feather headdress of the plumes of the same red bird. His long black hair was made into braids in which colored ribbons were entwined. These ribbons were so long and in such profusion that they trailed on the ground.

First the *chilan* purified the house by puffing on a thick black cigar stuck into a carved wooden holder. He then blew the tobacco smoke about to smoke out any evil spirits that might have been lurking there. He repeated this action as he walked around the magic square.

Entering the magic square, he sat down heavily on a wooden stool. A *chac* brought him a fire pot, and in this a charcoal fire burned brightly. From a small bag the *chilan* took out a little dry ground maize and some pieces of *pom,* the tree resin, or copal, which the Mayas used as incense. He dropped this on the coals, and it gave out an agreeable smell.

The boys were then made to come up in order. The girls followed. Into each of their hands the priest placed a little dry maize and copal, and as they passed by him each threw it on the fire.

After this the priest poured *balche* into a beautiful vase. This dark fermented honey drink was their wine. As he poured it he talked to a *kayum,* a man who assisted at the ritual. This *kayum* was to take the drink to the edge of Cobá. He was not to drink of it, nor was he to look back. When he got to the edge of town, he was to leave it there. Then any evil spirits which might still be about would follow him to the *balche.* They would then drink it and so would not return to harm the ceremony.

A *chac* now brought the priest his magic wand, a wonder-

fully carved wooden stick, with entwined serpents whose eyes
were inlaid in jade. Tied to the top of the wand were the rattles of a rattlesnake; a plant which gave out an odor of fresh
mint was tied around its shaft.

Then it was the turn of the Maya mothers to come forward
and with a new white cloth, woven especially for the ritual of
emku, cover the heads of each of their children present.

The priest went down the line of children, and over each head
he shook the magic wand nine times. He asked them if they had
kept the Maya customs; if they had respected their mothers and
fathers. He gestured as if to strike them as he would have if they
had not been telling the truth. If a child confessed to not having done the necessary things, the priest took him or her by the
arm and placed the child to one side.

When this was accomplished he sat down.

Now came the turn of the giver-of-the-feast. This "chosen
one" was a father whose son or daughter was participating in
the *emku* ritual. He was chosen by all the other parents to be
their representative. Since the ritual was very costly, no Indian
could afford to give it all by himself. All the families shared the
expenses, each giving turkeys, maize, or deer so that the cost
would not fall on one alone.

The giver-of-the-feast wore a newly made manta, woven by
his wife, who had made it as beautiful as possible. There were
wonderful designs woven into it: birds, monkeys, and slithering
snakes. He wore large jade earrings, and in a hole in his left nos-
tril (which had been made when he was a small child) he stuck a
yellow topaz. His face was painted with red-and-yellow designs.

In his hand he carried a hollowed-out leg bone of a tapir,
which was stopped at one end with black beeswax. Into it was
poured virgin water, water which had been caught in the leaves

of the forest and had had no contact with that in wells or lakes. This water was then mixed and tinted with flowers of the cacao plant. The giver-of-the-feast went down the line of children, anointing their heads and faces, even the spaces between their bare toes, with this virgin water.

While he did this not a single sound was uttered. The people and the children who were going through *emku* were so quiet that Ah Tok could actually hear the sounds of monkeys quarreling in the jungle some distance away.

At last the important moment came.

When Ah Tok was taking part in *emku*, he had not, at first, understood the reason for it, nor why his parents had been so grave while it was happening. His grandfather, the wise Ah Kuat, who often participated in such rituals, explained it. When a boy reached twelve years of age, he became, in effect, a man. As a child he had run about with neither clothes nor sandals. Whatever work he did was mostly play. Although he helped in the house or in the cornfields, it was a kind of play-help. Now, at the age of twelve, a Maya boy came of age. He would dress like a man and wear the *ex* and sandals. He would work like a man, and he would eat like one. Similarly, the girls would dress and work as their mothers did. The *emku* took place because parents wanted to see their children grow up and become real members of the Maya clan family.

Emku, which meant "the descent of god," had to be performed to every last detail. Nothing could be left out, for the gods must be pleased.

So the ceremony continued. The *chacs* came into the magic square with a small knife, and each in turn cut off the yellow topaz bead which all the boys had stuck to their forehead before this ceremony. Then the mothers of the girls came forward, and kneeling down before their daughters, they removed the sea shell which up till now had been the only article of clothing their daughters had worn. Now, each wrapped around her own daughter a beautiful skirt, which had been specially woven for the *emku* ceremony.

The removal of the shell was a kind of license to allow the girls to marry whenever it should please their fathers. And this they did after they were sixteen years old.

Now was the time for everyone to grow merry. The priest brought a large goblet which was filled with the powerful *balche* drink. While saying many witty things, which made those about him laugh, he gave the filled goblet to an assistant. This *kayum* was a singer, whose duty was to sing the chants and histories and help the priest in other ways. Now his duty was to drink the entire goblet of *balche* in one gulp. He was not allowed to stop even to take a breath, for it would bring bad luck if he did. All the people gathered about him, laughing and shouting as he drank. When he finished, they gave a big whoop. The drums began to beat and the flutes to chirp, and the people started to dance.

The children who had come of age were now given presents. The boys were given sandals, bow and arrows, a spear and, sometimes a flint knife, or *tok*. Hair ribbons, jade necklaces, and mantas were given to the girls. Some mothers even presented their daughters with a real loom, so the girls could weave clothes themselves. After the giving of gifts, all the people began to dance again.

THE WELLS OF CHICHÉN ITZÁ

THE ROAD to Chichén Itzá was very crowded as the Chen family continued their journey. The sixty-mile walk between Cobá and the next large city, was not terribly long, but even so it took two days. The glare of the hot sun hardly penetrated the greenery which covered the wide road. The road was still raised as a causeway. At several places where the land dipped down in a hollow the builders had managed to keep the road level. So at times the *sacbe* was more than sixteen feet above the land. Still, it was always straight, and it always kept the same width of fifteen feet.

It was obvious why the road had to be constantly repaired. In this fertile land seeds from the trees were always dropping down on the *sacbe,* and since only the smallest amount of earth was needed to make the seed sprout, the small plant soon sent its roots up through any tiny cracks in the road. And if it was not cut out before long, it became a tree and broke up the road as its roots grew and pushed up the rock.

Ah Kuat said there were roads like this all over Yucatán. Once when pursuing a deer, he had come across an old road which no one had ever mentioned. Partially grown over with trees, it led to ancient Maya stone cities, then all abandoned. But how long ago had this road been built?

As they continued along, passing people like themselves who were loaded down with things for trading at the market, Ah Kuat told the following old story:

"In very ancient times when their people had built the temples at Chichén Itzá and the other cities, there lived then a powerful lord. He was called Ucan. He made his kingdom so large that he found that he had to bind it together by roads, because being covered with stone, the earth of Yucatán was so rough that men could not travel easily or quickly over it. Ucan was so powerful a warlord that all he had to do to make a road was to carry a magical white stone. From this the *sacbe* unwound like a ribbon. The road made itself as he walked. So, in this way, he made many roads. He was so busy in all this, that unlike other Maya lords, he never married. In fact, he never even looked at a woman.

"But one day when he was building this road from Chichén Itzá, carrying his white stone and letting the road unwind like a ribbon, he met a beautiful woman. She had her hair rolled up and wrapped with gay, bright ribbons, as Maya women do. She was so beautiful that most of the other great Maya chieftains could not resist her. But Ucan paid no attention to her.

"'Ucan come here,' she said. 'Turn your face to me.' He paid no attention but continued to play out the road from the magic stone.

"But the woman was just as stubborn as he. She stepped in front of him, blocking his movements and bringing him to a halt.

"It is then that Ucan really saw her and how beautiful she was. He stopped, dropped the magic stone he was carrying, and began to follow her. After that he lost his power. The Mayas no longer built roads.

"The stone that Ucan dropped can still be seen near Champotón."

When Ah Tok asked if this story was really true, his grandfather laughed. These were moral tales to make young Maya boys realize the importance of continuing to work at whatever they were doing, no matter what happened. As for the age of the road, if Ah Tok had been able to read the Maya writing, he could have seen for himself.

At the beginning of the road were stone markers on which were written the various symbols of time. The time-marker had been put up in a period of the Maya calendar equivalent to 652 A.D. This made the road over 850 years old.

Yaxuna, the next city, was only a three-hour walk to Chichén Itzá. Now the road was more crowded than ever. Every once in a while a shout was heard, and the travelers would move away from the center of the road. A runner, the official message-carrier, was coming by. A message written on a piece of *huun*-paper, or beaten bark paper, was rolled up in his long hair and held there by a net.

Later, the people had to move aside for the procession of the Maya lords. First, they would hear the guards blowing the conch shells. The long mournful blast could be heard from far off. Then the warriors ran forward. As was the custom, their faces and bodies were painted in broad red-and-black stripes.

The spears they carried were tipped with flint points as sharp as metal. The spear shafts were covered with jaguar skin, and near the point were red-and-green cotton tassels. The warriors were bare-foot and bare-bodied, except for the *ex,* whose beautifully woven panels hung down to their knees in front and back. Through their pierced ears they wore long, smooth green shafts of jade. Each costume differed from the other only in the manner of helmets. One helmet resembled the open mouth of a jaguar; it was carved so skillfully out of hard wood that it seemed almost real. A spotted jaguar pelt covered the top. Another helmet had the head of a tapir; still another was like the skull of a man.

The warriors were followed by two trumpeters, each playing a different long, hollow note. Then more soldiers followed. Finally came the "True-Man," the greatest chieftain of the land.

He sat in a litter carried by eight men, four on each side, who balanced the poles on their shoulders. A feather canopy covered a framework of wood beautifully carved with twisting snakes.

Inside the litter, neither looking to one side nor the other, was the great man. He was dressed with a magnificent head-dress of quetzal plumes. These plumes, more than three feet in length, were so dazzling that they seemed to shoot out green-gold sparks in the sunlight. Around his neck was an immense

jade collar, and even his wrists were covered with jade ornaments. His earrings and the rings on his toes were also of jade.

He looked very proud, and as he passed, all the travelers
bowed and shouted: *"Halach uinic!"* When he passed, they
arose and touched a bit of the earth to their foreheads.

The True-Man was greater than all the other chieftains. He
served as a leader over several Maya cities. Revered as a god,
one of his titles was "The man of the greatest importance." His
word was final. It was law. The *batabs,* who were the gover-
nors of the cities, paid him careful attention. Even the high
priests did his bidding, for he was also head of the Maya
religion.

He had one wife, who was, in every way, his consort. It was
expected that his son would be someday as he was now—the
halach uinic. But if his sons were not worthy, his brother, the
uncle of his sons, would become the *halach uinic* after his death.

He was so exalted, so far above, so out of the reach of understanding, that Ah Tok could do no more than wonder at the
sight of him.

At high noon the travelers finally saw the great pyramid of
Kukulkan, white and dazzling in the noonday sun. They arrived
from the northwest, over *sacbe* number 6 (☉), as Ah Kuat said.
The road led first to a high stone wall which encircled all of
the sacred part of Chichén Itzá. Guarding the gateway were
soldiers who stood, spear in hand, watching all who passed.
Every once in a while, they would stop a traveler to examine
the things he carried on his back. Visitors from another province, who wore strange or different dress, were stopped and
questioned at the gateway. Since the city of Tulum had at the
time an alliance with Chichén Itzá, the soldiers allowed the
Chen family to enter immediately. Loaded down with goods,

all of them passed through the gate, following *sacbe* ●̣ , which led to the market.

Ah Tok had never seen anything as large as this *yaab,* or market, which was set in an immense plaza six hundred feet square. Around its sides, under a roof, were sculptured columns, carved with portraits of warriors armed with spears. This famous market, called by the people "the place of the thousand columns," contained numerous beautiful buildings. The sides were made of carved stones set together like a mosaic. Between the carvings the walls were painted red, yellow, and blue. Inside were the council rooms for the merchants, or *ploms.* These fat Mayas—the "possessed men"—had their own form of dress, which was very elegant. They had their own god, Ek Chuah, and in these stone buildings there was a shrine to him. They even had their own resthouses in the cities where they made their trade. They paid no taxes; that is, like officials of towns, they did not perform work-service.

As Ah Tok's father always said, trade was lifeblood to a

Maya. This could be easily understood. Since corn was the main crop, and a Maya farmer raised more than he could eat, his leisure time allowed him to create things of his own handiwork. Mayas became skilled craftsmen as well as farmers and, of course, each fashioned something distinctive.

Some, like Ah Tok's father, made blowguns. Others made spears or feather headdresses. The women made all the pottery, and they did all their own weaving, not only the family's garments, but also the cloth which was used as part payment of the family's tribute-tax. Even then, there was much cloth left over, and this was then used for trade to get something else they did not have. Mayas who lived in the high forests hunted birds for their feathers, which were exchanged for food or jewels. Jadeworkers carved the sacred stone which all Mayas loved. Others were woodcarvers. Then there were the salt-gatherers. The finest and purest salt in all the Americas was gathered in the salt lagoons of Yucatán near the sea. At high tide the lagoons filled. After this, the Indians dammed up the entrance so that the water could not retreat into the sea. Under the hot rays of the sun the water evaporated, leaving a thick layer of white salt. The Indians only had to scoop it into sacks. Salt was needed by people who ate cereals or grains. The Maya chieftains who ruled the lands near Ekab knew this. They controlled the salt, and they were known as "the lords of the sea."

All this and much more was brought to market. It was amazing how orderly it was. There were more than ten thousand people there; yet everyone who came to trade knew where he was supposed to go. His stomach bulging over his loin cloth, a fat official directed the new arrivals according to what they had to sell or trade.

Those who sold food were in one section. Under cotton awnings which shielded them from the burning sun, women sat, offering corn in sacks. Little hot red peppers, like fire in the mouth, were sold in little piles. The women kept arranging them after a would-be buyer had fingered them. Also sold were sweet potatoes and a tuber called *macal,* which was like a potato. There were tomatoes and squash and many types of beans. The fruit market was large, but the Indians ate the fruit then and there because it was difficult to carry.

In another section sat the spice traders, who offered salt, pepper, an herb called *chaya,* and other similar things. Vanilla was also sold. Any Indian could tell where this part of the market was because of the sharp scent of the vanilla orchid. These beautiful white blossoms gave out a deep heavy scent; when the blossoms died, a podlike capsule formed. This vanilla bean looked like a dark, dried stringbean, and it was used by the Mayas to flavor honey or chocolate. Women also made a perfume out of it.

In another section of this wonderful market of Chichén Itzá people sat under their white awnings, offering cloth in every form that a Maya could possibly wish for.

And there were also the jewelers, highly respected men. They sold the popular jade and the topaz, a small yellow stone which some called "amber." These yellow stones were worn by men in a hole which had been bored in the side of the nose by a very painful operation. Some Mayas liked to wear jade inlaid in their teeth. The jeweler took a bone drill, which he whirled back and forth on the front of the tooth until he had made a deep hole. Into this he cemented a small round piece of jade. Also offered here were jewels made of sea shells, turquoise, or obsidian, and sometimes even pearls. But only the "possessed men," those rich with cacao beans, could afford to buy them.

These very rare pearls were as large as one's thumb. They had been brought a thousand miles, all the way from Panamá, by the Maya sea traders.

The image-makers had a busy section in the market. Their place was near the stone buildings where the *holpop,* the judge of the market, sat. Here a Maya could buy an image—in clay, stone, ceramic, or wood—of the god he wanted. Many of these clay images were cast in molds. A farmer could buy little images of Chac, the rain god, easily recognized because he had a long snout for a nose. His eyes were T-shaped, like falling tears. The farmer placed these clay gods in the soil, hoping they would help bring the needed rain.

The most beautiful image of all was of Yum Kax, the corn god. At least the farmer thought so. He was made to appear very young, his headdress was a sprouting corn plant, and he was represented holding a pot which also held a flowering plant. Clay images of him were always put into the soil of new cornfields.

There was a large trade, too, for the image of the god of travelers. Everyone who walked the roads—and all did on occasion—carried the image of the god of the North Star in their little net bag. He protected all travelers.

The busiest and noisiest section in the place was the slave market.The hubbub resulted because the great men, the merchants and the chieftains, were bidding for them. Slaves, called *penta,* stood at the bottom rung of the social ladder. In the market they sat with their hands tied behind them, their hair all shorn.

Such was the way they were always pictured in Maya books in stories of war and slave-making. Most *penta* were Mayas who had been captured in battle, for Mayas were always fighting with each other, city against city, province against province.

When a warrior captured an enemy in battle, that man became his personal property. He could use him in work, or he could sell him. The slaves were mostly Mayas, but sometimes peoples of other tribes were captured. Men were also made slaves because they had committed crimes. Stealing was considered a serious crime. All people who lived in clans were supposed to be of the same blood, one large family. They had no doors on their houses. When someone stole something from another, he was immediately judged to be anti-social. If the crime was small, he could repay the damage by work. If the man stole again, he was put into the slave market, for the Mayas had no jails.

If a man killed another, even by accident, he had to forfeit his own life. If he gave offense to the gods, he was sacrificed. Maya justice was swift and final.

Slaves were in demand by the great traders, who needed them to carry their trade goods or to paddle their dugout canoes. The merchants, who carried tall walking sticks, were there in crowds. Orderlies fanned them with large feather fans. Flies were many, for the merchants had their hair perfumed with a sticky, smelly oil that attracted insects.

When a slave had been looked over and it seemed that he would be fit for hard work, the merchant paid for him in cacao beans. The merchant's servant wore a *hotem,* a bag attached to his waist, which contained brown cacao beans. He counted out a hundred beans, for this was the slave's price. A man could pay for anything he might want to buy, with cacao beans. Thus, chocolate, or *hā,* served the Mayas both as drink and as money. When a Maya received chocolate in the form of cacao beans, he was careful to press and rub each bean, for some Indians

made false bean-money by removing the hard skin and filling it with sand. This was considered a serious crime.

This day, an Indian was on trial for passing spurious bean-money. Within one of the carved stone houses, on the side of the market plaza, an Indian sat with his arms tied behind him. On a dais that was covered with a woven mat sat the judge. He listened to both sides of the story; from the man who had received the false money; from the man who had given it. If found guilty, the giver of the money could be put into slavery. If he had not known that it was false, he would have to pay the man.

In the afternoon the market ended. The Mayas folded the white awnings, packed the foods they had not sold, and all went off toward the great pyramid.

To enter the sacred plaza they had to pass alongside the Temple of the Warriors. At its base were many square columns, whose carved figures represented warriors, standing erect with shield and spear. Covering these was a roof made of huge wooden beams that had been carved and painted to depict battle scenes of the past. This led to the Temple of the Warriors.

Steps led up the sides of this small flattened pyramid to the temple. At the gateway were immense carved stone serpents, their open mouths painted red and green. The thick stone bodies rose twenty feet into the air, and at the very top were the rattles of a rattlesnake.

In front of this temple in the plaza stood the greatest pyramid in Yucatán. It was so large that all else seemed to be nothing beside it. Ah Tok had heard about the pyramid of Kukulkan all of his young life. Now he stood in its shadow. A tall pyramid, over 125 feet high, it was faced with beautifully carved and laid stone. There were four wide stairways which faced the cardinal directions: north, south, east, west. Each had ninety-one steps, and on their sides, running from bottom to top, were the same immense snakes as at the other temple. Their bodies formed the balustrade or railings of the stairway.

Ah Tok found that the tread of the stone step was so high that he could not lift one foot above the other if he did not use his hands. This, of course, was not allowed. A Maya Indian must climb erect, without stopping and without using his hands. At the very top, at the apex of the pyramid, was the sacred temple. Ah Kuat said that inside this pyramid was another, older one.

The city of Chichén Itzá was very old. People had first come there because of its great wells. It was founded, some said, in 452. Then for some unknown reason it had been abandoned. In the tenth century, the Itzás had come down from Mexico. They were of a different people. They had come to this place and found it deserted. Many of the old buildings still stood, so they rebuilt the pyramid.

Then between the years 987 and 1185, the Toltecs also came from Mexico to Chichén Itzá. This was the time of Kukulkan, the great giver of laws and the god of the winds. He ordered the pyramid rebuilt again. And the new was put over the old. In his honor the people named it the Pyramid of the Plumed Serpent.

But because the people always remembered the old things, the builders put a secret stairway inside. Ah Kuat heard that within it there was a secret chamber, the Red Jaguar Throne Room. Here stood a life-size figure of a jaguar, carved in stone. It was painted a fiery red. Its "spots" were said to be made of seventy-three disks of polished jade.

The games began later in the afternoon. There were seven ball courts in Chichén Itzá, and in these they played the game *pok-a-tok*. On this day, the festival of Kukulkan, the game was being played in the great court. Although it was crowded with people, still they could not obscure the size of the court.

This great ball court stood at the east end of the plaza. Those who wished to watch the games had to climb sharply inclined steps to the seats. It was only as one sat down on the stone seats that he really got an idea of the enormity of the playing field. It was 545 feet long and 225 feet wide. When he leaned over the wall, Ah Tok realized that he was more than thirty-five feet above the ground. The entire court was made of stone, and around its base were carvings of the figures of warriors. The roof and sides of the two small buildings where the judges and chieftains sat were also covered with carvings.

Pok-a-tok, the only game played here, was so ancient no one could agree as to when it had begun. Even Ah Tok's grandfather, who seemed to know everything, could not say from whence it had come. Some thought it had begun with the Olmec tribe, who lived north of the Mayas. In olden times, 1,500 years ago, they

and the Mayas had been deadly enemies. Now the Olmecs were gone, extinct. But in the land where they lived, in the moist warm jungle, the rubber tree grew. They called it *olli*. And *Olmecs* meant "the rubber people." Perhaps this was because they had rubber. Indeed, they were the first to make a rubber ball for this game.

All that Ah Tok's grandfather knew was that *pok-a-tok* was played by all the Mayas as well as other tribes to the north and to the south. A Maya from Tulum, who had paddled his canoe upriver into some inland lakes called Nicaragua, had once told Ah Kuat: "Even there, the people play the game with rubber balls."

Pok-a-tok was played with ten players on each side. Clad in an *ex* and sandals, they also wore thick gloves and protective coverings on their hips and elbows. The object of the game was to butt—with elbow or hip—the rubber ball through what some called a "basket." Except that it was no basket at all, but rather a large round stone. In its center was a round hole, a foot in diameter, just large enough for the rubber ball. The stone basket was set into the stone wall, twenty-five feet above the playing field. But it was placed perpendicular so that it was very difficult to get the ball through the hole.

In the shadows of the late afternoon the players ran back and forth passing the ball which bounced off their hands. They kept jumping and butting the ball, trying to pass it through the stone basket. Everyone was naturally very excited. Men were betting for this team or the other. One man bet ten slaves against another's ten slaves; some bet their jade against another man's gold earrings. Some even gambled away their house. Ah Tok's grandfather thought it was quite immoral and very "un-Maya" for the chieftains to do all this in front of the common Indians.

But it was the custom.

The plays began after the ball game. There were so many different things going on at the same time in the great plaza that at first one did not know what activity to attend. Naturally, everyone in the Chen family seemed to want to see something that the other did not want to see. Yet no one could miss the Dance of the Reeds, mainly because it took up so much space.

At one side of the Platform of the Skulls the musicians were beating out a rhythm. Ah Tok had never seen so many instruments together at one time. Three Mayas were playing the *tunkul,* the large upright drum that came up to the drummer's chest. It was beaten by hand. Another drum, which lay on the ground, was really a hollowed-out log, beautifully carved. It had two tongues of wood, which were beaten by sticks that were rubber-tipped. Other players had a sort of drum made out of a tortoise shell. When struck with the palm of the hand, it gave out a sad and doleful sound.

Then there were the trumpets. These were made of clay and were very long, almost as long as a man was tall. Other Indians played flutes, made either from reeds or from the leg bones of a deer. Another kind of music was made by several Indians who had copper bells tied to their legs and arms. They merely jumped up and down and the bells gave out a tinkling sound. Other musicians used rattles, large gourds that had been glued to a long stick. Inside the gourds were hard seeds; outside, they were decorated with ribbons. Ah Tok found that he could not keep still. His feet kept moving to the rhythm of the lively music.

The Dance of the Reeds was performed by 150 Indians in a wide circle. The signal was given by the *holpop,* who was beautifully dressed in a blue-and-red woven manta and a headdress of red parrot feathers. As well as being a judge of the market, he was "the keeper-of-the-musical-instruments." When he gave the signal, all of the dancers began to move in time to the beat of the drum. Holding arms, they moved to the right like a giant turning wheel. Each held in his arms rubber-tipped lances. The *holpop* clapped his hands and two dancers left the circle. They represented the hunter and the hunted. While the circle of Indians moved, the two in the center jumped about so that the other could not take good aim. When one threw his rubber-tipped lance, the other not only had to escape it, but he was also expected to try and catch it as it whirled through the air.

Later the Chen family drifted with the crowd toward a stone-built platform, which lay halfway between the Temple of Kukulkan and the well of sacrifice. Although it had an official name, most people called it the Platform of Venus, because carved on its sides were the symbols of the planet Venus. It was a square platform, not more than ten feet high, with four sets of stone steps that led to its top. Here the Mayas enacted their plays and their comedies.

Tonight, people wanted to be gay. Tomorrow was a solemn

day, the day of sacrifice. The Maya lords knew that their people were worried, for so many things had been "happening" in the last years. The worst, of course, was the appearance and disappearance of the white men. Each time they returned they came in greater strength. Those who read the oracles still could not agree on who these unknown people really were. Tomorrow they would try to find the truth and beg an answer from the gods. But tonight they were to be gay.

The actors were masked, as actors always played their parts in masks. If a man played the part of a water lily, then his mask was made to look like such a plant. Sometimes the actors played very serious roles. If they played the part of a god, they came masked as that god appeared to the Mayas. They believed that when a man played a god, he was a god. So, for the Maya, acting and plays had real religious meaning. This night, the actors made fun of Maya customs. The comedy of the *Cacao-grower* always made them laugh. It jested about their consuming passion—chocolate.

An actor appeared as a cacao plant. His body seemed to be a tree, and from its trunk, grew cacao pods. As "chocolate," he wanted to know why he was so loved; thus, he went to a market. People were using him for money. One actor was masked as an old woman. She took the cacao beans, or "chocolate-money," from another actor who was buying. Like all Mayas, the old woman rubbed the bean to see if it was real, not just a skin filled with sand. When she did this, insects came out of the skin. How the audience laughed when newly born mice fell out of other skins! Different, unexpected items continued to come out of the skins. So the actor playing the part of the "chocolate tree" shook his branches in despair and left the market. Other comedies followed. All dealt with someone in Maya life. They poked fun at the *Parasite,* the *Pot-maker,* the *Chili-vendor.* . . .

It was so late by the time that Ah Tok and the rest of the Chen family were ready to go to the resthouse, that they had to be guided there by torches.

THE WATERY ANSWER

THE DRUMS were beating. They had begun even while the sky was still dark. The beat became louder and louder as drummers in temples throughout Chichén Itzá took it up. The throbbing was loud enough to awaken both gods and men. Yesterday had been a joyful day—with market and games, plays and comedies, and a procession of buffoons. Today, it was different. It was the day of the watery sacrifice.

It had not rained for several months. For some reason Chac, the rain god, had withheld the gift of rain. But most upsetting of all was the coming and going of the unknown men, the "bearded ones." Like all other Indians, the Mayas feared the unknown. It inspired distrust. Many believed that the lack of rain and the coming of the strange men were somehow connected. Perhaps the gods had not been given what they wanted.

The gods created and controlled the world. They did not simply give rain, sun, or plants to a man. He had to ask for what he wanted, and in order to get it, he had to give a sacrifice to the gods—burn incense or food, or best of all, shed human blood for them. In turn, the gods traded their withheld gifts of rain, sun, or plenty.

Ah Tok knew this was true. Once when he was about to kill a turkey with an arrow, he said, half aloud, to the god of the animals that he had made an offering of incense. He reminded this god of what he had done, so that the god would then allow the turkey to be killed by Ah Tok. And it was.

The greatest sacrifice a Maya could give to the gods was a human life, provided, of course, that it was someone else's life. It was very important that the one about to die should realize the great honor he was doing himself by giving himself to the gods. If he made a noisy fuss about being sacrificed, it caused very bad luck. The gods would then think that the other Indians did not want to give him in sacrifice or that the man himself was doing it with a lack of grace.

The one to die this day was a girl. For several weeks she had been given the finest Maya foods; she had been waited on as if she were the chieftain's wife. The finest mantas were hers to wear, as well as jewels of jade, gold, and turquoise. One of the powerful *batabs,* the governor of Chichén Itzá, was giving this girl in sacrifice. He was doing it reluctantly, for her going gave him great pain. But it had to be done. The gods must give answer to the things that troubled everyone.

The sun had lightened the sky. Thousands of people began to gather in the plaza. Directly in front, that is, north of the pyramid which had the stairway leading up on its four sides, was the sacred road. It was thirty-three feet wide and nine hundred feet long. Its surface was whitened every day with white lime to make it bright and clean.

This ceremonial *sacbe* led to the *cenote* of Chichén Itzá, the largest natural well in all Yucatán. Everyone, including pilgrims to this sacred city or those who had visited the market the day before, stood along the road.

Because Ah Kuat was known to some important old men of the city, the Chen family had a place near the edge of the *cenote*. It was one of the good places.

The procession came along the road. First were those who carried the incense. From clay fire pots which they held before them a thick smoke poured forth, rising into the still air. It was the odor of the gods. Then came the priests, wearing newly made robes which had been made from bark-paper, the very same paper that was used in making Maya books. The only decoration on their ankle-length robes was a row of bright shells sewn to the hem.

The priests were followed by the rulers of Chichén Itzá, who were carried in litters on the shoulders of Indians. Then followed the girl. Her body was painted blue, since this was the color of sacrifice. It was called "Maya blue" because the Mayas loved to paint the walls of their houses with it.

After walking the length of the sacred *sacbe,* they came to the edge of the natural well. It was a circular one, two hundred feet in diameter. The limestone walls had fallen in over a long period of time, and by now its vine-covered sides were almost vertical. Trees hung over it, and large iguanas, with long green tails, ran up and down its sides.

The water lay sixty-five feet below the surface. Its pale-green color obscured the bottom of the well, which lay another thirty feet below the water's surface.

When Chichén Itzá had first been founded in 452, the well had been used for drinking water. Then the city had been deserted for four hundred years, and when it was inhabited again, the water was no longer clear. It had probably turned green from the algae in it, which, of course, had not been removed all those years. So this well could no longer be used for drinking water, and thus it became the well of sacrifice. The people of Chichén Itzá used another *cenote,* Xtoloc, for drinking purposes. It lay in the older part of the city, and to get to the water, two masonry stairways wound down its sides.

At the very edge of the well of sacrifice was a small temple, which had several rooms. In one of them incense smoke poured out from a hole in the wall. Around the sides of the *cenote,* the masons had carved seats in the living limestone rock.

The drums beat a slow sad rhythm as the priests, with upraised arms, asked the gods for an answer. Why did rain not fall? Who were the strange people who were coming to their land? How were the Mayas to deal with the strangers? Would the gods give an answer?

The girl who was to be the messenger to the gods was now deprived of her jewels and her fine clothes. When her legs and hands were bound, two priests took her by her limbs, swung her back and forth, and when she was over the side of the well, they let go. Her body made an arc in the air and then splashed into the water and disappeared. A great cry went up from all the people. All present took something they loved most—a jade necklace, a piece of gold, a copper ax—and flung this possession into the water of the *cenote.*

Then the enormous crowd of people dispersed. They moved so silently that one could only hear the soft patter of their feet. It sounded like softly falling rain.

Later in the day, Ah Tok began to ask questions of his elders. As they packed their goods to return to Tulum he kept asking his father or grandfather—anyone who would lend him ear—what had happened. How were the priests to know the answer? When would it come?

Well, in the dark of the evening the priests would climb down to the water level to look for the girl they had sacrificed. If she were still alive, they would have from her a "watery answer." The words she spoke would be those with which the priests could then foretell the future.

And what if she did not come to the surface? What if she was dead and could not come back?

No one had an answer for this question, but they did know that such a happening would be very bad fortune for the Mayas.

Ah Tok realized again the multitude of things one had to know in this life. There were so many customs to remember, so many rituals that had to be understood.

Later, most of the people seemed to learn the answer at the same time. The Chen family, loaded down with new things that they had traded for at the fair, were halfway home when they heard the terrible news.

The girl who had been flung in the well at Chichén Itzá had not returned to the surface. There had been no reply from the gods.

The priests gave prophecy . . . Mayas would be soon faced with terrible events.

AGAIN, THE "BEARDED ONES"

LIFE SEEMED to go on at Tulum as it always had. The people still went to their cornfields. The wives and daughters of each house wove the garments for all the members of the family. People still worked hard. They still paid their taxes with goods and work-service. Trade went on, and life went on.

However, in Ah Tok's family, life was not the same. Ah Kuat, the wise old grandfather, had become very ill on the family's return from Chichén Itzá so many months ago. He was eighty years of age, which was incredibly old for a Maya. Being a *chac*, Ah Kuat had seen many things, and he had read many things. So when he became ill, he knew death was upon him.

The Mayas believed that disease was brought by someone who had laid a spell on them. It was thought, too, that winds could bring diseases.

97

The Chen family had called in the *ah man,* who was both a curer and a warlock, or sorcerer. Supposedly able to make disease disappear, he was also considered able to send disease to someone else. This witch doctor came to the house of a sick person with his fetish bundle. He took out an idol of Ixchel and put it beside the ill one. In his bundle, he also had the jawbone of a tapir, some herbs, and the tail fins of a manatee. After perfuming the house with incense, he blew tobacco smoke over the patient. Then out of his bundle, he took his *ām,* which were six magical stones. He rolled them out on the floor as if they were dice, and then he put his nose close to them to "read" what they said. The pattern they took was believed to tell the path of the disease. A witch doctor did not like to try curing an illness unless he was certain that he would be successful. If the ill one died, the family might decide that the witch doctor should die as well, to accompany the man he helped to send to the other world.

The curers had all sorts of plants and herbs that they also used to help cure disease. But Ah Kuat was now beyond all these.

Now came a priest called the *pocam.* He had been summoned to hear the dying man's confession. This was important. If he knew anything that he had done to cause his death, he must say so. He must confess, or else other members of the tribe might die also. Upon his death Ah Kuat might go to any of the thirteen heavens or nine hells that formed the Maya underworld. But so long as he had kept the Maya way of life—that is, doing what customs said one should do—he would on his death go to stay under the "first tree of the world." And there he could drink all the chocolate he wanted.

The actual place in the underworld where one went after death, really depended on what one did during life. Warriors and mothers went to the first heaven. Fishermen went to a heaven of their own. Those who took their own lives went to a special heaven; suicides even had their own goddess, Ixtab. She was always pictured as a woman hanging with a rope around her neck.

Finally, Ah Kuat died. His body was wrapped in a shroud made of his own cotton manta. The family placed some ground maize and a few jade beads in the dead man's mouth. "This was done," it was explained to Ah Tok, "so he could use the jade for money. Then he would not be without means to buy something to eat in the other life."

A grave was dug in the mud floor of the house, and the dead grandfather was lowered into it. In the grave Ah Tok's mother placed a beautiful dish filled with corncakes, and another large bowl filled with *balche,* "the wine of the country." The dead man was also provided with some of his books, the books with pictures and symbols in which the Mayas read their history. When other men died, they were treated similarly. If a man had been a fisherman, his nets and his harpoons would be buried with him. If he had been a great warrior, the dead man would be laid to rest with his shields, spears, and headdress.

It was thus explained: "They should not be without something in the other life."

The great chieftains, of course, were buried differently. When a famous *halach uinic* died at Chichén Itzá, they buried him in the temple. He wore his jade, his pearls, and gold. Women were slain in his tomb to serve him in the other world. The ashes of famous war captains were put into life-size jars. These were made in such a way that the head-shape on the jar resembled the face of the war captain when he was still living.

All the members of Ah Tok's family would eventually be buried in the floor of their house. When all the available space was completely filled with graves, the rest of the family would move away and build another house elsewhere. The old house would then become a family shrine. Ah Tok knew this very well. His grandfather had often gone on a pilgrimage to the ruined city of Mayapán, where the Chen family lay buried. There old Ah Kuat would pay his respects to his ancestors.

In the month of Pax, which to the Mayas was the month of war, the white men returned again. In the year 1518, the people of Tulum heard it from the Indians who had just paddled their canoes from the Isle of Cozumel. The foreigners came now in four large vessels with many bearded men aboard and the unusual animals, which the strangers called "horses." Having informed Tulum, the Indians paddled quickly to the south to tell the news to the people of the next province.

The next day, the *nacom,* the war captain, of Chetumal province came to Tulum. He arrived with more than fifty canoes, each filled with forty warriors. These Indians had come painted for war, their bodies covered with broad red-and-black stripes. They carried spears and arrows, horns and conch shells.

Brought up from the beach at Tulum on a litter, the *nacom* was carried about the small plaza. He alighted in front of the main temple and walked up the steps to meet the governor of Tulum. This was no ordinary war captain. His eyes were blue, his beard long and blond. But like the Indians, his body was painted; his ears had been slit and were stuffed with jade earrings. His nose had been pierced in the custom of the Maya, and through it he had stuck the bone of a chieftain he had killed in battle.

This unusual *nacom* let it be known that the white men who were in Cozumel were no gods. They were men, just as the Mayas were. The white men had come for women, for gold, for slaves, for conquest. They were, of course, able to kill others, but they could also be killed themselves. They were not gods; they were Castillians. And how did he know all these things?

Well, he was one of them himself. For the war captain of the province of Chetumal was the famous Gonzalo Guerrero. The Mayas here all knew his story. When he was first captured by the Mayas, they had made him a slave. But since he was wise in the ways of warfare, he had fought and won many battles, and the Mayas of Chetumal had made him their war captain. He spoke their language, married a Maya woman, had Maya sons. He tattooed his face and prayed to Maya gods. He *was* a Maya.

Once again, as they had done so often in the past years, the Mayas were to become soldiers. Although there were really very few Maya men who did not usually do another kind of work, when war came upon the land, the Maya men were soldiers too. Their weapons were always kept in the house, ready for immediate use.

All who could fight must do so. The boys who were not yet soldiers, were to go into battle as weapon carriers. Their duty was to supply the spearmen with spears, the archers with arrows.

Within five days, the Maya armies, consisting of all those who were allied to each other, had reached Campeche. In order to reach this city, which was on a straight line from Tulum, they had used the *sacbe*-roads. Traveling on a *sacbe* was faster than by canoe.

Champotón (then called Chakampoton) lay right on the sea. The buildings of this large Maya city were built as close to the sea as at Tulum. Offshore was a small island on which there could be seen a large pyramid, white and gleaming, just as old Ah Kuat had often described. This had been built in memory of Kukulkan's departure from the land of the Mayas to return to Mexico.

Beyond the small island four ships lay at anchor, the ships of the bearded men. They did not seem very large to Ah Tok from where he stood. It was only when the Maya canoes approached them that he realized the strangers' ships were many times the size of Maya dugout canoes.

Over fifty war canoes began to encircle the ships. Then came a noise like thunder and a flash of fire, and one of the canoes turned over. The Indians shot their arrows, making the ships look like a porcupine with its quills. On board ship, the white men had two Maya Indians whom they had captured the year before. These two captives began to speak in their own Maya language to the warriors in the canoes. They said that the bearded men came from a land greater than Yucatán and that their king was very powerful. They wished the Mayas no harm, and they asked permission to come ashore and fill their empty water casks.

So the Castillians came ashore.

The Mayas had been told what to do. They helped them find water. But Maya warriors were gathered in the thick woods. It was all part of the *nacom's* plan. Gonzalo, now the Maya war captain, sat there, watching the men who had once been his countrymen.

The Maya warriors were divided into groups. Each group had a banner, a flag made of feathers. On it was the symbol of their own tribe.

First, there were the archers. They used a great bow, a *chulul,* almost as tall as themselves. As they had to use both hands, they had no shield. Instead, they wore a protective covering something like armor. It was a quilted cotton jacket made of strong fibers, which had been soaked many days in salt brine to be toughened; it was so strong that arrows could not enter it. This jacket, the *euyub,* covered the chest and the entire left arm, the bow arm of the archers.

The spearmen wore such a quilted covering from neck to ankle. Their helmets, made of wood or tapir hide, were decorated with animal heads. Their long spears had a sharpened flint-point with a cutting edge like a knife. They used a spear thrower, a wooden board into which fitted the arrow. It gave a greater force in throwing. Each spearman carried ten or more spears, and Ah Tok and the other young weapon carriers had to supply them with new spears in battle.

Next in the battle order were the swordsmen, who came into battle at close quarters. They had long, flat wooden swords, edged with obsidian. This black volcanic glass cut like a razor; in fact, the Mayas used them as such. Hence, this sword was particularly effective in hand-to-hand combat.

All swordsmen always carried shields, some of which were made of the large shell of the sea turtle. Others were covered with the thick hide of either the tapir or the manatee.

Then came those who used the sling, or *yuntun.* This was a long piece of woven cotton material, both ends of which were held in the hand. In the center, at the greatest width of the cloth, was the place for the stone. The slingers whirled the *yuntun* around their heads, released one end, and the stone— the size of a duck's egg—went straight and fast to its mark.

There were still other weapons. Older Indians, who could no longer fight with spear or sword, carried wasps. The wasp nests, larger than the size of the rubber ball used in the game of *pok-a-tok,* were wrapped in a strong cloth. One could hear the wasps, strident and angry, buzzing within the cloth. Wasp nests were hurled into the places of retreat used by Indians who refused to come out and fight.

Now was the time of ambush. Everything was quiet, for this was the war the Mayas fought best—surprising an enemy. The *nacom* sent out his scouts, who were called "road weasels" because they moved along silently and kept so close to the ground.

The Castillians saw the Indians. They formed themselves into a square . . . and waited. Now the Indians blew conch shells and sounded their clay trumpets. The slingers released a hail of stones which gave out the noise of a clapped bell as they bounded off the steel helmets and armor. Those who had no helmets and were hit on the head, fell to the ground. Under the hail of stones, the spearmen crept forward. As they came to one knee they brought back their arms. The air was suddenly filled with the noise of spears swishing through the air. Many on the other side were killed, and many wounded. As soon as they hurled one spear, they crept nearer and hurled another.

It was then that the Castillians replied, firing weapons which Ah Tok had heard about, but had never seen. They sounded like a thunder clap, followed by a flash of fire. Many Indians were instantly bowled over, but the enemy were unable to load their "thunder sticks" as fast as the Indians could throw spears. And now the archers went into action. The sharp twang of the bowstring filled the air.

The Castillians could not stand up to this attack, for there were only two hundred of them as opposed to thousands of Mayas. As the foreigners retreated the swordsmen rushed in for close action. But the white men were brave too. Their swords were of metal and greater length, and they knew how to use them well. Many a Maya warrior died without his head.

Still the Mayas would not hold back. At this point, the Indians discovered which man was the white men's captain. He was tall, blue-eyed, and had a short blond beard. Although he had been wounded in the mouth, and blood poured down the side of his metal armor, he still fought and continued to direct his men in battle.

The Indians began to shout: *"Halach uinic! Halach uinic!"* They used the name of their supreme Maya lord, for in their minds this wounded one was, indeed, the *halach uinic* of their enemy. And the Mayas wanted to capture him alive. They always tried to capture the other side's war captain. Since a *nacom* always went into battle beautifully costumed, he could not be mistaken for anyone else. The object was to capture him, because the Mayas believed that once their leader was caught, the warriors lost confidence. The leaderless warriors then believed that the gods had sided with the enemy, and they themselves could not win. So they threw down their shields and ran. When an Indian hung his shield from his back and dragged his spear, it was called *cuch chimal,* meaning "surrender." The Mayas also used the word to mean "cowardly."

But the Mayas were not cowardly now. They went forward to try and capture the white men's captain. Many died. Still they came on. At this point the Castillians used their horses, animals which none of the Maya warriors except the *nacom* Gonzalo had ever seen. The men sitting on the horses carried long out-thrust spears, and they rushed down on the Indians, impaling them before they could run away. Some who were not killed or wounded by weapons, were knocked down and trampled by the horses. For these were war horses that had been trained for battle, trained to trample their master's enemy under their hoofs. Keeping this in mind, the wise *nacom* had ordered the Maya to erect barriers of trees, and dig ditches into which they could place sharpened sticks. Those Indians who were able, ran behind the barricade, and the horses tumbled into the trap.

A new sound filled the air, the sound of the Castillian trumpet. It looked like a Maya trumpet except that it was made of metal. The long note it sounded meant "retreat." The white men began to fall back, fighting the Mayas, who followed them all the way to the beach. The Indians were shouting; their conch horns were blowing as they rushed on the enemy.

Flinging themselves into their small boats, those white men who could not find a place inside, hung on the gunwales and were dragged along in the water. Now their warships lifted anchor and began firing the large cannons aboard. But even this did not stop the Mayas. Even though many died, they continued the fight. For the men they were now fighting were the "bearded ones" who had haunted their lives all these years. The Indians were frantic with the feeling of victory. Some went into the water and hurled their spears; others swam after the boats, holding flint knives in their mouths to use when they reached the escaping enemy.

Now came the turn of the gods. Those white men who had had the ill luck to be taken alive were brought into the city of Champotón. Their hands were tied behind them; their bodies were painted blue. They knew what was to be their fate. The Maya gods had given their people victory. Now the Mayas must thank them and give them the offerings which they believed the gods loved best.

The Maya warriors were very proud of what they had done. Those who had captured the enemy alive were allowed to wear parts of them as trophies. After boiling his victim's head and removing the flesh, a Maya warrior might take the dead man's jawbone and tie it to his own arm. In the eyes of the wearers of these trophies, such warriors were considered very brave. They drank heavily of *balche* at feasts in their honor.

A word of warning now came from their *nacom*. Gonzalo told them that the Castillians, though few in number, would return. The white men were very brave, and they were very persistent. So now the Indians must all work on their defenses. If the enemy were ever allowed to get their horses on hard ground, they could defeat a whole Maya army. No matter how brave the Mayas were, they would be defeated. It was a thing to remember.

And the white men did return the very next year in the month of Ceh, the New Fire month—February, 1519, according to the Spaniards' time. Shortly before this, Ah Tok had reached the age of seventeen, and he had made plans to be married. For then it was the time of 2 Ahau 8 Zac, and this had been marked as Ah Tok's "lucky year."

After the severe defeat of the "bearded ones," no one expected them to return so soon. So Ah Tok's father, the *tupil*, had arranged his son's marriage to a very beautiful girl named Ix Cakuk. They had gone to the priest who read before them the *Book of Days*.

The Mayas believed that all life was influenced by the stars and planets. There were good-luck days and bad-luck days. Thus, the priest had to consider if Ah Tok's birthday was a good day for Ix Cakuk, and did not conflict with her's. And the priest thought that her birthday did not conflict with Ah Tok's, and that her name was a good one. Names were considered very important to the Mayas. At birth everyone was given a name, or *paal*. The prefix *Ah* was placed before each boy's name; the prefix *Ix* was placed before each girl's name. Hence, whenever anyone mentioned the name of another, every Maya knew at once whether it was a man or woman who was being spoken about.

So the marriage had been arranged. "When a Maya man thinks of marriage," Ah Tok's father had told him, "his own father must take good care that the girl will be of good family and of good quality." Since it would have been bad custom for either Ah Tok, his father, or even his mother to speak to the girl or her family, they had used a matchmaker.

The matchmaker, an old woman, had gone to the girl's family and had told them of Ah Tok's good qualities and of the high standing of his family. When it was done, the two families had exchanged gifts. A time had even been set for the marriage, but now . . .

This time the Castillians had returned to the Isle of Cozumel with eleven ships. The Indian who brought the message to Tulum, said that five hundred white men had been counted at Cozumel . . . and there were many horses. This time they had not made war on the Indians. Instead, their chieftain, a short man with a full, square beard, treated everyone with kindness. He seemed to know a few words of the Maya tongue, and he was able to ask about the white men whom the Indians had kept captive.

The Indian messenger then unrolled from his hair a piece of paper on which words were written. They were a message which he had been told to deliver to any Castillians he found.

When the Indian arrived at Tulum, he had delivered the message to Gerónimo de Aguilar. Curious about what was hap-

pening, many Mayas had followed the messenger until he found
Gerónimo, who was working at the house of the governor of
Tulum.

The Spaniard had also sent a present of glass beads along
with the message. To the Mayas, who had never seen glass before, these beads looked like their highly treasured jade.

Gerónimo accepted the letter and then looked at the glass
beads. He gave the beads to his master, the lord of Tulum,
who seemed very pleased to have them. Then Gerónimo asked
permission to read the letter. Sitting down, he read half aloud:

> "Noble Sirs;
>
> having departed from Cuba with a fleet of eleven ships
> and five hundred Spaniards, I have reached Cozumel, from
> which place I write you this letter. The inhabitants of this
> island have assured me that there are in this country five
> or six bearded men who are in every way like ourselves,
> but they cannot give me any further description of them.
> But from what I hear, I conjecture and I feel sure that you
> are Spaniards. I and these noblemen who come with me to
> settle and discover these lands beg you earnestly to come
> to us without any delay or excuse within six days from
> the time you receive this. If you come to us, we shall all
> acknowledge and be grateful to you for the good services
> which this fleet will receive from you. I send a brigantine
> in order that you may come here to safety."

The letter was signed: *Hernando Cortés.*

After Gerónimo finished reading this, he asked his master
for permission to visit his friend Gonzalo, the *nacom* of Chetumal, and show him the letter. While the lord of Tulum was

wondering whether or not he should allow Gerónimo to go, another messenger came with a second note. This one read:

> Gentlemen and brothers . . . I have learned that you are
> captives in the hands of a cacique. I have sent soldiers and
> ships and a ransom . . . Come in all haste and you will be
> welcomed and protected. I am here at Cozumel with five
> hundred soldiers and eleven ships, in which I go, if God
> wills it to a town called Chakampotón.

Since Gerónimo had always been a faithful slave and had
helped his master to win battles with other Maya chieftains, he
was allowed to go. After a half day's canoe trip to the south,
he arrived at Chetumal. He was received there by Gonzalo, who
was now a greater *nacom* than ever, having defeated the enemy
in the battle of the year before. Of this, nothing was said. In
reply to Gerónimo's suggestion that they both go to Hernando
Cortés, Gonzalo replied:

"Brother Aguilar, I am married, as you know, and have three
children. The Indians look upon me as a *nacom,* a captain in
wartime.

"Look at me. I have my face tattooed and my ears pierced.
What would our countrymen say when they saw me in this
way? And, besides, look how handsome these boys of mine
are. But you go, and God be with you!"

Gonzalo's wife was listening to this conversation. And although the men were speaking in Spanish, and she could not
understand their words, she realized the import of all the talk.
In Maya language she said to her husband: "What right has
this slave coming to you, my husband, and talking to you? Go
off with you!" she said, turning to Gerónimo, "and don't trou-
ble us any more with your foreign words."

And this he did. Returning to Tulum, he received permission from his master to visit his countrymen. He got a canoe and gave an Indian a present to paddle him to Cozumel. Ah Tok stood there with his father, watching the canoe as it disappeared into the rough waters of the open sea. Somehow the feeling came over him that even though Gerónimo had been a slave and was now going back to his own people, he would neverthe-less have something to do with the Mayas' future. When the canoe was out of sight, Ah Tok turned back.

"It is *xul,*" he said . . . which meant: "It is *finished.*"

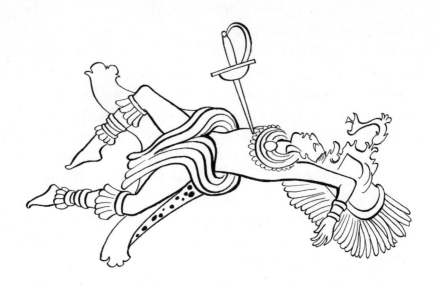

"XUL"—IT IS FINISHED

AND SO the Maya way of life was finished. It did not, it is true, end all at once. In fact, it was a long time in coming to an end.

For those eleven ships and five hundred men sailed away from Yucatán, and many believed that this was the last anyone would see of them.

Then there had been a battle at Cintla, in the province of Tabasco, where cacao was grown. Tabasco was close to Mexican territory. The captain Cortés landed horses there, and when the Indians came down upon him, he ordered the cavalry into battle. Thousands of Indians were killed. The chieftain surrendered and offered the white captain anything he wanted. He gave up his maps and his tribute charts showing the towns who gave tribute to another great chieftain, a man called Moctezuma, who was the Aztec emperor of Mexico.

The white men sailed north in direction of the Aztec empire. And now the Mayas heard, for such news travels fast, that Gerónimo, who had been merely a slave at Tulum, was now a great man. He rode a horse, he wore fine clothes and steel armor, and he sat by the side of the white captain Cortés.

Many of the Maya lords were content; they could not—according to an expression used by Ah Tok's father—see a jade set in their nose. This meant, of course, that they were blind to things that were going on about them. They were happy to be rid of the white men, who would now fight the Aztecs. Then both sides, Spaniards and Aztecs, would kill each other off. Or so the Mayas thought. They felt they would be able to rid themselves of both enemies without even having to fight.

Then the Mayas began to war again among themselves. They fought over this little thing and that. The Maya lords were spending their strength when they should have been arming to save themselves.

Besides, the white man had left behind an enemy to fight for him—smallpox! One of the sailors had had the disease and had infected the Mayas with it. The Indians had never had small-pox before, but now the disease spread like fire going through dry grass. No witch doctor was able to prevent it. Thousands died of it. It was so horrible that the priests recorded it in their books: "In katun 2 Ahau was when the skin eruptions took place, the time that the pustules occurred. It was the *maya-cimil.*" *Maya-cimil* meant the "easy death"; warriors who would have preferred dying in battle, died instead from smallpox.

Meanwhile, the white men left them in peace. But then in 1521 the terrible news became known that the white men had conquered the Aztec capital. And Moctezuma, the great Aztec emperor, was dead.

In 1524 Hernando Cortés returned to Xicalango in Tabasco province. He came with soldiers, horses, and buffoons. The former Maya slave Gerónimo, who was now known as Gerónimo the translator, accompanied Cortés. The Spanish leader had not come to war with the Mayas, but had only come to find and punish one of his own men. This man had been sent by Cortés to found a colony in Honduras, which is south of Yucatán. Disobeying the order, he had set up his own government instead.

Once again, the Maya lords thought that they would help the white men just enough so that the two parties would kill off each other. Hernando Cortés was allowed to walk right through the country of the Maya. Not one Indian raised his voice; not one raised his spear.

In 1527, eight years after Captain Cortés had first come to Yucatán, eight years after Gerónimo had left it, a slave no longer, the Spaniards came again. This time it was for war. This time it was for the conquest of the Mayas. A Spanish captain, named Francisco de Montejo, landed 380 men and fifty-seven horses at the coastal town of Xelha. After killing all the Mayas there, he then blocked the *sacbe*-highway. Now no warriors could come from the interior, as they had done before, to fight the enemy.

Still the Mayas fought. Every place in which the white man set foot he was defeated, and Spanish graves began to appear on the beaches of Yucatán.

So the white men left this region and went south. They sailed into the great bay of Zamabac, in the province of Chetumal.

Once there, they contacted Gonzalo, the *nacom*. In answer, he wrote them letters, pretending that he was still a captive. Go to such and such a place, his letters said; there are no Indians there. Under the impression that Gonzalo was helping them, they went to a place near the sea. Here Gonzalo had hid his warriors, and the white men were so badly beaten that they all left, and by 1535, there was not a single white man in all of Yucatán.

So they went on to Honduras. Here in the warmer lands, where there are rivers and the cacao beans grow, the Mayas had trading stations. The Spaniards took these easily and began their conquest. But as soon as Gonzalo heard this, he got together a large armada of canoes, and with a thousand warriors he sailed south to give aid to the Indians.

It was April, 1535. The Spaniards had made a fort out of logs and were trying to keep back the attack led by Gonzalo. One of the Spanish soldiers was able to identify Gonzalo out of the group of Indian warriors, who all seemed to them to be "brown and noisy." The Spaniard took aim, fired—and blew Gonzalo Guerrero's head off.

The Spaniards kept up the fight and the Mayas resisted fiercely. Captain Montejo, aged and full of scars, gave up, and the Mayas thought that this would be the end of the wars. But it was not. Montejo's son, also a captain, took up the fight where his father had left off.

The year 1542 was a dreadful year, with one battle after another. The Spaniards killed every Maya they saw; the Mayas killed every Spaniard who fell into their hands. The cities were neglected. Plants and even trees began to grow on top of the temples. The roads became overgrown, and many of the corn-fields were no longer used. The old people complained that all the young men thought about was fighting. The merchants complained that no one cared as they once had about trade. People still carried on their way of life, but they could never do

anything in peace. No one knew when the Spaniards would come, out of nowhere, riding in on those terrible snorting horses to destroy all the Mayas.

As this dreadful year continued, all over the land chieftains were surrendering; warriors were turning their shields around their necks and dragging their spears. Every month another Maya city gave in to the invaders.

By 1546 it was all over. T'iho, near Chichén Itzá, was a large city full of stone buildings. One day, Captain Montejo marched into the city with a great red-and-gold flag—the flag of Spain with its lions of León and castles of Castilla painted on it.

He took possession of T'iho and all the land around it in the name of the king. He said that this city would be his capital, and he would name it Mérida. He chose to call it this because there was a city in Spain with that name. That city had once been occupied by the Romans, and like T'iho, it had many buildings of white stone.

The Spanish soldiers began to tear down the Maya temples in order to build houses for themselves. Soon the city had churches and dwellings, and the Indians were scattered far and wide. Both sides had fought for what they believed to be right. The Spaniards truly believed that it was their mission to bring their way of life and their religion to the Mayas. It was the Mayas' duty to resist, and they bravely did so, up to the very end.

But now the life of a great culture had come to an end. The Spaniards would not allow the Mayas to go back to their old cities. Fearful that the Indians would turn again to their religion and make war again, the Spaniards made them settle in new places.

Now the Mayas no longer built great towering pyramids; nor did they build gleaming white roads. No longer did they wear wonderfully large feather headdresses and feather costumes. The priests either disappeared or were killed. Some still wrote in their books to keep alive a memory of their history; but this was done only in secret. One day, when the Spaniards discovered that the Indians were still consulting these old books, they gathered them all together. At the city of Mani they made a large fire, and one by one they burned the ancient books. As this was being done, all the people cried aloud. The old culture was dead.

Yet, a part of this culture was still alive. Deep in the interior was El Petén, a place with a large lake and thick jungle. And here a tribe of Mayas—the Itzás—maintained their old way of life.

A tribe of Itzás had been living in Mayapán, the capital of the Mayas, when it was destroyed during the civil war. Realizing that the city could not be rebuilt, they decided to leave. One night, after the priests had gathered up their ancient books, thousands of Itzás left the city and marched for ten days through marshes and jungle. Finally, they reached the shores of Lake Petén, surrounded by a jungle filled with ruins of old Maya cities. Close by was Tikal, the greatest of them all.

It was the year 1460 when the Itzá-Mayas began to build their city on an island in Lake Petén. They cultivated the land around the lake and built temples. They continued to practice their religion and the Maya way of life. When the Spaniards first came in 1502 the Itzás knew about it. And when they came in 1517 the Itzás knew about it. But the old men of the tribe thought that if they did not go to war but remained where they were, no white man could find them. After all, they had the jungles to protect them. Even though they knew that all the old Maya cities were being captured, they still did nothing.

Then the war was over. The Yucatán warriors were made into slaves, and those who escaped went to El Petén. Thus, the Spaniards discovered that there was still another tribe of Mayas alive and in full strength.

For years the Spaniards tried to conquer them. Once some white men even got as far as the city, where they saw pyramids and temples just as there had once been in Yucatán. The Maya lord was very friendly and invited them to come inside the city. Then, when they were all there, a signal sounded and his warriors surrounded them. The next morning their hearts were offered to the sun god.

One hundred and fifty years after the Mayas of Yucatán had yielded up their country to the invaders, the Itzá-Mayas were still living the old form of life.

But all things must come to an end. In 1697, a large force of Spanish soldiers came to the lake. There was a short battle. The Mayas fled or were killed. And that was really the end of the Maya culture.

A POINT OF HISTORY

WHEN ONE reads a re-creation history it is always helpful to know what is real and what has been invented by the author. In this book the only fictional element is the placing of Ah Tok in a specific time and place. Many boys like Ah Tok did live among the Mayas, however, and carry that name. The rest of *Maya. Land of the Turkey and the Deer* is based on documents which have been known and used by scholars for many years.

Gerónimo de Aguilar and Gonzalo Guerrero were real men, and this their history! In 1511 a Spanish captain named Valdivia was sailing his ship from Panamá to the Caribbean island of Santo Domingo. On board he had a crew of forty men and a treasure of twenty thousand golden ducats. As the ship approached Jamaica, where there are shallows called *Las Víboras,*

or "the vipers," it struck an exposed reef and sank. Twenty men
lived to escape in one small boat that had neither sails, water,
nor food. Half died in the first days; the boat then drifted to the
Isle of Cozumel.

This island, ten miles off the eastern coast of Yucatán, was
a sacred place to which the Maya people made pilgrimages. Of
the ten survivors, four, including Captain Valdivia, were sacrificed. All the others died of illness except Gerónimo de Aguilar
and Gonzalo Guerrero. They were made slaves and were owned
by the Maya lord of Tulum. Gonzalo Guerrero—*guerrero*
means "war" in Spanish—went quickly into a Maya tribe,
married a Maya woman, and adopted Maya dress and customs.
He became a *nacom,* a war captain. Gerónimo de Aguilar, who
had studied for the priesthood and was of a more peaceful
nature, become a docile slave, but he kept green the memory
of his own land by reading a breviary. In this religious book he
was able to keep track of the flight of time and the Christian
feast days.

In February, 1519, Hernando Cortés arrived in Mexico with
five hundred men and eleven ships. In Campeche, to the north,
he had heard Indians shout the words: "Castilian. Castilian."
It was then that he wrote the letter quoted in this book. After
that, Gerónimo de Aguilar was brought to Cortés, given clothes,
and made a member of the expedition which set off for the
conquest of Mexico.

Cortés went on to Tabasco, the most northwesterly province
of Mayaland. A battle took place and when Cortés routed the
Indians, they sued for peace and brought him as a gift a very
attractive Indian girl whose name was Malinal. She had been
born in Paynala, twenty-five miles from the coastal city of
Coatzacoalcos. Since her father had died when she was young,

she was given as a slave to a chieftain in Tabasco. So when Tabasco was conquered, she was then given to Cortés. Now Malinal, or Doña Marina as she was called by the Spaniards, spoke both Aztec and Maya. And Gerónimo de Aguilar spoke the Maya language, as well as Spanish. The Conquistador Cortés would speak Spanish to Gerónimo, who then translated into Maya, and Marina would translate the Maya into Aztec. In this way Cortés passed on his plans and ideas, and through this "triple cascade of translations," the conquest of Mexico was paved.

No one knows what the Fates held for Gerónimo de Aguilar in the end. However, in the archives in Seville, Spain, there is a document which reads: *Information of the services and well-deserved merits of Gerónimo de Aguilar and other persons of his family.* Many of those who took part in the Maya conquest or who wrote about it mention the history of Gerónimo. The best known is that of Francisco Cervantes de Salazar's *Chronicle of New Spain* (Second Book, Chapters XXV–XXXIX, pp. 110–122, Madrid, 1914).

The discussion of the *emku* ritual is based entirely on the account in A. M. Tozzer's edition of Bishop de Landa's *Relación de las cosas de Yucatán* (Peabody Museum, Volume XVIII, Cambridge, Mass., 1941).

V. W. VON H.

Begun at Hacienda Uxmal, Yucatán (1959)
and completed in Lima, Peru, April, 1960

	MAYA WORLD	CENTRAL AND SOUTH AMERICA
	First farmers arrive at Guatemala, Chiapas, and Yucatán, 2000 B.C.	
B.C. 500–1	Rise of Maya civilization, about 350 B.C.–A.D. 300	
	Development of astronomy; invention of calendar and writing	
A.D. 1–500	Maya culture spreads: period of prosperity, 300–700 Building of great stone cities; stone time-markers Tulum, 433	
	Chichén Itzá, first built 452	
500–600	Intellectual center at Copan	
600–700	Sculpture reaches highest development	
700–800	Mayas number 3 million	
800–900	Drought causes widespread death, abandonment of cities in Yucatán, Mexico, 890	
	Mayas reoccupy older coastal cities; paper books	
900–1000	Chichén Itzá occupied by Mexicans led by Plumed Serpent God, 987	
	Kukulkan (Plumed Serpent God) proclaimed ruler and god of Mayas: achieves unity and peace, 987–1017	
1000–1100	Architectural development of Chichén Itzá: temples; great pyramid; ball court Mayapán founded	
	Kukulkan returns to Mexico, June 23, 1017	
1100–1200	Chichén Itzá destroyed; Mayapán becomes chief city of Mayas	Aztec migration begins, 1168
1200–1300		
1300–1400		
1400–1500	Mayapán destroyed, 1441: warfare among tribal states (decline of Maya civilization)	Rise of Aztec civilization
	Itzá-Mayas settle at Lake Petén, 1460	Aztec and Inca civilizations at height
1500–1600	Spanish explore and conquer Caribbean and northern South America Maya traders meet first white men, 1502	
	First white men reach Maya coast, 1511	
		Cortés conquers Mexico, 1519–1521
	Spanish conquest of Mayas, 1527–1546	Pizarro conquers Peru, 1531–1535
	Maya temples destroyed; Indians forced to resettle	
1600–1700	Itzá-Mayas conquered at Lake Petén, 1697	

	NORTH AMERICA	EUROPE	NEAR EAST AND ASIA
B.C. 500–1		Golden Age of Greek civilization	Confucius in China
		Alexander the Great conquers known world to India, 336–323	
A.D. 1–500		Roman Empire controls Mediterranean, including Near East, 116	
		Final division into Eastern Roman Empire (Byzantium) and Western Roman Empire (Rome), 395	
500–600		Beginning of modern Western European civilization	Byzantine Empire advances
600–700			Arab Empire begins, 632
700–800		Moslem defeat at Tours, 732, stops Arab expansion into Europe	
800–900		Charlemagne crowned emperor of Holy Roman Empire, 800	Golden Age of Arab Empire, 750–1258
900–1000	Eric the Red discovers Greenland, about 985	Arab rule in Spain at height	Second great advancement of Byzantine Empire
1000–1100	Leif Ericson visits Vinland, about 1000	William the Conqueror invades England, 1066	
		Crusades against Moslems in Holy Lands, 1096–1270	
1100–1200			
1200–1300		Magna Charta in England, 1215	Mongols overthrow Arab Empire, 1258
1300–1400			Ottoman Empire (Turks) founded, 1288; overthrow Byzantine Empire, 1453
1400–1500		Renaissance Invention of printing, 1439	
	Columbus discovers America, 1492	Moors expelled from Spain	Vasco da Gama reaches India, 1498
1500–1600	Beginning of Spanish explorations in New World		
	Ponce de Leon discovers Florida, 1512		
	Balboa discovers Pacific, 1513		
	Magellan voyages around the world, 1519–1522		
		Turkish expansion into Europe stopped at Vienna, 1529	
	De Soto discovers Mississippi River, 1541	Protestant Reformation	
1600–1700	Pilgrims land at Plymouth, 1620		

BOOKS FOR FURTHER READING

Andrews, Edward Wyllys, "Dzibilchaltun: Lost City of the Maya," *National Geographic Magazine,* January, 1959, Vol. 115, pp. 90–109.

Gann, T. W. F., *Glories of the Maya.* New York, Charles Scribner's Sons, 1939.

Malkus, Alida, *Dark Star of the Itzá.* New York, Harcourt, Brace & Company, Inc., 1930.

Morley, Sylvanus Griswold, "Excavations at Quirigua, Guatemala," *National Geographic Magazine,* March, 1913, Vol. 24, pp. 339–361.

————, "The Foremost Intellectual Achievement of Ancient America," *National Geographic Magazine,* February, 1922, Vol. 41, pp. 109–130.

————, "Chichén Itzá, an Ancient American Mecca," *National Geographic Magazine,* January, 1925, Vol. 47, pp. 63–95.

————, "Unearthing America's Ancient History," *National Geographic Magazine,* July, 1931, Vol. 60, pp. 99–126.

————, "Yucatán, Home of the Gifted Maya," *National Geographic Magazine,* November, 1936, Vol. 70, pp. 590–644.

Parsons, Elsie Worthington (Clews), ed., *American Indian Life, by Several of Its Students.* New York, B. W. Huebsch, 1922.

Ryan, Marah Ellis, *The Dancer of Tuluum.* Chicago, A. C. McClurg & Company, 1924.

Scoggins, Charles Elbert, *The House of Darkness.* Indianapolis, The Bobbs-Merrill Company, 1931.

Squier, Emma Lindsay, *Bride of the Sacred Well, and Other Tales of Ancient Mexico.* New York, Cosmopolitan Book Corporation, 1928.

Stephens, John Lloyd, *Incidents of Travel in Central America, Chiapas, and Yucatán,* 2 vols. New Brunswick, Rutgers University Press, 1949.

————, *Incidents of Travel in Yucatán,* ed. with intro. by Victor W. von Hagen, 2 vols. Norman, University of Oklahoma Press, 1960.

Thompson, Edward H., *People of the Serpent.* Boston and New York, Houghton Mifflin Company, 1932.

von Hagen, Victor W., *Maya Explorer, John Lloyd Stephens and the Lost Cities of Central America and Yucatán,* 4th ed. Norman, University of Oklahoma Press, 1960.

————, *The Ancient Sun Kingdoms of the Americas: Aztec, Maya, Inca.* Cleveland and New York, The World Publishing Company, 1960.

————, *The World of the Maya.* New York, New American Library, 1960.

Willard, Theodore Arthur, *Kukulcan, the Bearded Conqueror.* Hollywood, Murray and Gee, 1931.

————, *The City of the Sacred Well.* New York, Grosset & Dunlap, Inc., 1931.

————, *The Wizard of Zacna, a Lost City of the Mayas.* Boston, The Stratford Company, 1929.

INDEX

ABOUT THE AUTHOR

VICTOR W. VON HAGEN'S many expeditions in Mexico and Yucatán, most of the countries of Central and South America, the Galapagos Islands, and the West Indies have made him a recognized authority on the great Indian cultures of this hemisphere.

Mr. von Hagen is the author of more than thirty books, including *The Sun Kingdom of the Aztecs* and *The Incas: People of the Sun,* both for young people. These two, with *Maya,* comprise his trilogy on the major cultures of the Western Hemisphere before the coming of the white man.

ABOUT THE ARTIST

ALBERTO BELTRÁN is a young Mexican artist whose artistic abilities and understanding of the ancient Indian cultures of his native land have already earned him a reputation as "the successor to the late Miguel Covarrubias." The Panamerican Prize, the highest distinction in the drawing division of the First Biennial of Painting and Drawing, was recently awarded him by the Instituto Nacional de Bellas Artes in Mexico. He is known in this country for his fine work in *The Sun Kingdom of the Aztecs* by Victor W. von Hagen and other books.